William George Ward

Capital And Labour

William George Ward

Capital And Labour

ISBN/EAN: 9783744726009

Printed in Europe, USA, Canada, Australia, Japan

Cover: Foto ©ninafisch / pixelio.de

More available books at **www.hansebooks.com**

CAPITAL AND LABOUR:

A PAPER READ BEFORE THE LITERARY SECTION AND GENERAL
MEMBERS OF THE NOTTINGHAM AND COUNTY LIBERAL
CLUB, AND TO DELEGATES FROM OPERATIVES'
TRADE SOCIETIES,

BY

W. G. WARD, ESQ.;

ALSO

SEVEN NIGHTS' DISCUSSION

THEREON,

BETWEEN CAPITALISTS, TRADES' UNIONISTS, REPRESENTATIVE
WORKMEN, AND OTHERS;

AND

MR. WARD'S REPLY.

CHAIRMAN, MR. WILLIAM WHITEHEAD.

NOTTINGHAM:
PRINTED AT THE "DAILY EXPRESS" STEAM PRINTING OFFICES, VICTORIA STREET.
1874.

EXPLANATION.

As the Chairman presiding at these Readings and during the intervening Discussion, I am desired to explain that both Papers and Speeches have been revised, and here reprinted, by direction of the Committee, in compliance with numerous earnest applications for complete copies in book form, not only from members of the Club but from many others also. At the same time, I may be permitted to acknowledge the uniform and marked kindness and courtesy of all parties, not only to myself but to each other, during the entire debate.

WILLIAM WHITEHEAD,

CHAIRMAN OF COMMITTEE.

Thurland Street, Nottingham,
October, 1874.

CAPITAL AND LABOUR.

INTRODUCTORY PAPER, BY W. G. WARD, ESQ.

(TUESDAY, MARCH 31, 1874.)

THE subject of the paper I am about to read is "Capital and Labour."
A very extensive and important subject it is, involving the interest and
welfare of every human being. I should not have presumed to address
you on so great a theme of my own accord, but having been specially
requested to do so, I cheerfully comply, and will do my best to deal
honestly and fairly with some of the aspects of the subject which appear
to me to be important at the present time ; and when I have concluded I
hope that I shall have shown a spirit of candour and impartiality which
will be a proof of my good intentions. I do not appear as the champion
of my own or of any class. I shall not seek to please the great, nor to
gain the applause of the multitude. The aim of men in providing and
obtaining that which contributes to, and constitutes, temporal welfare,
cannot succeed without the co-employment of both labour and capital,
which are mutually dependent on each other and their interests are, in
the main, identical. I do not mean that it is possible for all antagonisms
to cease ; I do not think they will or can. It is natural and inevitable
that they should arise, but they should be dealt with in a spirit of charity
and forbearance on both sides. No lengthened injustice can exist on
either side, without those who sow the wind reaping the whirlwind.
Unless a fairly just advantage be gained on both sides the one will desert
the other, and leave it to its own helplessness. I need not say a word as
to the powerlessness of capital without labour, but it is not so needless to
ask what labour can do without capital. The ploughman cannot wait
until harvest for the food by which he lives. If he has not saved some
himself, and to that extent become a capitalist, he must have what others

have saved ; so also, the labourers who make the plough, or dig the iron
ore from the ground, or the coal which is necessary to smelt it, must be
fed and clothed and housed ; capital supplies all these wants, and is thus
absolutely necessary to production.   Again, what can labour do without
the tools and machines used in all manufactures, or how could what one
man produces be exchanged for something else that he wants, without
navigable rivers, canals, and railways ? or how could the surplus wealth
of one country be exchanged for the surplus wealth of another without
ships, and harbours, and dockyards ?   The comfort and convenience of
every one's daily life depend on the savings from the results of past toil,
and capital is simply a fund reserved from consumption—the produce of
previous labour.   Those who have saved nothing could not even live
from day to day without help from the savings of others ; and they
would be utterly powerless to carry on the production and commerce
upon which their future comfort depends.   Is it not right, therefore,
that the benefits arising from the joint action of capital and labour should
be shared by both in a spirit of friendliness ?   There is a feeling abroad
of bitter antagonism between the two, and many people appear to think
that the capitalist is the natural enemy of the worker ; that the division
of society into two classes, rich and poor, is a social injustice needing
prompt redress.   The justification, however, of this state of things lies in
the simple acknowledgment of the fact, that he who has justly earned his
wealth shall keep it, and enjoy all legitimate advantages arising from its
use ; and not be robbed of it by those who have been idle and not earned,
or who, having earned, have squandered their earnings.   Equality is impossible so long as men differ in capacity, in industry, and in prudence.
John Ruskin puts this point very clearly.   He says:—"If a man does
not eat his cake to-day, he ought to be allowed to have it, without
grudging, to-morrow ; and this principle is antagonistic to equality.
This is the great law of property—that if a man works for a thing he
shall be allowed to get it, to keep it, and consume it in peace."   And I
may add, that if he chooses to employ it to produce further wealth he is
entitled to his fair reward.   But it is said, capital takes the lion's share.
I venture to submit that capital does not command a very large proportion of the profits arising from transactions in which it is employed.
There is a fundamental error here into which many fall, which consists

in supposing that capital and labour are the sum total of what is necessary to the production and distribution of wealth. Brain work, anxiety, knowledge, inventive genius, administrative skill, and a never-resting commercial activity, are elements which must not—nay, cannot—be ignored. The instances of large, apparently excessive, remuneration falling to the lot of certain individuals, are mainly due to the possession and exercise of some of these rare qualities ; but there is no monopoly, no interference with the fiercest competition, in these matters. For a few who appear to achieve a disproportionate success, how many succeed but indifferently, and how many fall in the race ! the public, consequently, must be held to have the advantage of these gifts or qualities at the cheapest possible rate. In looking at the large fortunes sometimes gained by single individuals in England, these considerations must not be over-looked ; and it ought not to be forgotten that capital—pure and simple—obtains a less rate of interest in England than anywhere else. If any one desires to lessen the profits of English manufacturers and merchants, I think his best chance of doing so will be to bring an increased competition to bear in the matters of inventiveness, in the practical development and application of inventions, and in general administrative capacity and the art of economical management. "The jewel cutter, whose sight fails over the diamonds — the weaver, whose arm fails over the web—the iron forger, whose breath fails before the furnace—know what work is ; but not more than the inventor or the merchant, whose brain is always on the rack, and whose life-blood ebbs away under the constant harrass of anxiety and thought." So far as the rich are idle, they are justly open to reproach ; but there are also *idle* poor. My observation leads me to believe that neither can be successful. If all *work*, and only on that condition, they may expect success ; and I believe that, in the main, it will be found that those will be the most successful who can give to the community the benefit of that class of work which is the rarest, and which can extend its influence over the largest area of benefit. That is the class of work to which I have been referring, and the price of bodily labour or ordinary skill will take its rank accordingly. The only test as to whether a profit is legitimate or not, depends upon whether it is for a service rendered, and high and rare service will ever reap a high reward. Peculiar genius, if directed to the production of something the public wants, or can enjoy—or to the improvement or cheapening, by a better process of manufacture, that which is required—may command, does command, and always will command, a high rate of reward, to which practically there is no limit. So also, the skilful organisation of labour, so as to employ it to the greatest advantage of the public, the managing and carrying out of efficient systems of trade, the forethought and enterprise which lead to sound speculation as to the future necessities of the public, may all yield large profits without the slightest injustice to the labour employed. But if all I have said be admitted, there would still be antagonisms between the two classes of employers and employed. It is not easy to adjust their respective claims. It is said by the theoretical political economist, that each is entitled to what he can obtain, and that the laws regulating supply and demand will, in the long run, redress all injustice. There is much truth in this, but there still remains the further question as to whether it is not possible to deal with such temporary wrongs as arise from time to time either from ignorance or selfishness on the one side or the other. I must consequently proceed to speak of Trades Unions and Federations of Employers. So far as the object of trades unions is to raise the working classes in the social scale, and on their behalf to resist oppression and injustice, my sympathy is entirely with them. The vast number of working men is the measure of the importance of their welfare. And I fully believe that their interests cannot be secured and protected single-handed. Combination is, therefore, justifiable, and even praiseworthy. No property can be more sacred than the faculties of a man's mind, or the powers of his body, and he has a right, in any way he thinks proper, to set his own price on his services, so long as he does not injure or interfere with the freedom of others. On the question of wages, I am of opinion that the interests of the State demand that they should be as high as they can be legitimately and fairly maintained. This is essential for public tranquility and attachment to the institutions of the country, to enable parents to educate their children, and the only security against famine in bad times, which has ever been the fruitful cause of discontent and rebellion. Famine, or even deep misery, and the noble virtues of patience and resignation, do not go hand in hand, and those who have nothing will not submit to starvation without attempting to seize on the property of others. A man must have something at stake to make him recognise the great primal and fundamental laws by which society is held together. All men should have an interest in acknowledging the rights of property. I say, then, that workmen are fairly entitled to combine in trades unions, to resist all unjust aggressions and tyrannies of employers, to endeavour to regulate wages, where necessary, on equitable and just principles, and to establish, as far as possible, good rules and regulations ; such, for instance, as that all wages for good work shall be paid in money and without deductions of any kind. For such objects I think a strike, if fairly conducted, and if all other means have failed, is perfectly justifiable. There are other important functions which come within the scope of such societies. They ought to provide for relief in sickness, pay to members out of work, assistance in cases of accidents, old age annuities, death payments, loss of tools, and emigration. And they ought to develop systems of co-operative banking and working, which, in my opinion, will, in the end, prove the great lever to secure proper wages and to limit excessive profits wherever they exist, and so adjust the differences and settle the rival claims of employers and employed. The funds for these various dissimilar objects ought to be kept separate from each other. Provident investments intended to provide for future unforeseen calamities and the inevitable necessities of old age, ought not to be used to further what may be regarded as trade interests ; and investments of savings, whether in co-operative banks, or businesses, or manufactories, should be sacred. So far as funds may be required to further the claims of labour, they should be specially raised for that purpose, and should such funds accumulate, as they often do in the hands of trade societies, they should never be locked up, but invested in such a way as to be forthcoming in cases of emergency on the shortest possible notice. Having conceded, without the slightest reservation, the right of men to band themselves together to further their common interests, to put their own price on their labour, and to withdraw their labour from the market—or, in other words, to strike—if they think fit ; admitting, freely, that the rapacity, greed, and injustice of employers in many instances afford a full justification for such a course,

I must now emphatically condemn many of the acts which have been in the past more or less associated with trades unions. Molestation of employers and damage to or the destruction of their property, I might dwell upon, but I shall proceed to speak more at length of those acts which have been directed against the personal freedom and the liberty of individual action of other workmen. In the supposed interests of labour, acts have been committed which the better class of workmen cannot but regard with detestation and abhorrence ; and which even the promoters and perpetrators of, dare not attempt to justify. I suppose most people will at once concede that all actual violence is a crime. I go further, and fearlessly assert that so also is any attempt at persecution, any intimidation, in short, any annoyance whatever. They strike a blow at freedom, and are an unwarrantable tyranny. It is very difficult to draw the line on these points. In some cases it may seem impossible to define where persuasion pure and simple and honest ends, and where persecution begins ; but, at all events, we may be quite clear about the principle. I know perfectly well that I am now on delicate ground. Nothing is more debateable, and in fact nothing is more keenly discussed now-a-days, than the laws which have been directed against these very abuses. I may specially refer to the Criminal Law Amendment Act. I should condemn myself for moral cowardice if I did not do so. I, therefore, unhesitatingly say that I believe it to be over-stringent in some respects, and unjustifiable so far as it would touch acts when committed by trades unionists, which it could not reach if committed by other people. I do not, however, advocate its unconditional repeal, without having something substituted in its place. In the sacred name of liberty, I claim a full and sufficient protection for every individual. I know that individual liberty has often been trampled in the dust, and the most cruel coercion exercised in the interests of trades unions, and they must, therefore, not complain if it be sought to keep them to their just and proper influence, and within the bounds of what is fair and right. If a hundred men may combine, as I contend they may, to set a price on their own labour, it by no means follows that they should be allowed to dictate to fifty others, or to one other, the price which they shall demand. The national instinct for personal freedom will be found to be strong enough to claim and to insist that coercion and intimidation shall not be allowed to over-ride individual liberty. There may be, and I believe there is, very great difficulty in attempting to define intimidation and coercion, but the difficulty of the task must not cause it to be abandoned. If it be true that "Britons never shall be slaves," then they must be protected from every tyranny, including the fear of their fellows. I am glad to find that Her Majesty the Queen has been graciously pleased to appoint a Royal Commission to inquire into, and report upon, the whole of this subject ; and I have no doubt that in consequence much light will be thrown on the true state of the case, and particularly on such acts as picketing, watching and besetting men who accept situations which have been left by trades unionists on strike. It is contended, on the one hand, that such acts do not in the remotest sense imply coercion, and on the other that they create fear, and thereby exercise an unfair influence. This is a point worthy of the keenest, most minute, and careful consideration. I shall venture to commit myself to the opinion that where previous persuasion has evidently failed to induce workmen to join the unions or to take part in a strike, such acts ought not to be allowed during its continuance ; they seem to imply an interference with the right of a man to dispose of his labour as he thinks fit, and if that is so, they are certainly without justification. My observation and knowledge of actual facts leave me no room to doubt that abuses of a very grave character arise from the practice of picketing. I must not be understood to object to the simple attempt to exercise persuasion, or to the giving of information, but to such molestation or obstruction as arises from persistently following, besetting and watching, with a view to create such a fear as may cause a man to abandon work which he has voluntarily accepted. What I want is that labour shall be free—free to combine or free to be independent, and the laws so framed that every man shall be able to do exactly as he likes with his labour. If he thinks it desirable, either single-handed or in combination with any number of others, to leave his work, let him ; but I claim that he shall be securely protected from being compelled or frightened into doing so by any man, or any set of men. The power which men gain by combining in trades unions is very great. I think that they are entitled to it, but they have no right to exercise it unfairly to the injury of other men. Let the golden rule of the right to freedom work both ways. Whilst claiming

for themselves freedom to combine, let them not deny to others freedom
to be independent. Let them "Do unto others as they would have
others do unto them." I now leave this point, and shall proceed to say
a few words on several matters where I think the action of trades unions
is founded on a mistaken policy. I think the limitation of apprentices
and learners is unsound and unjust. It is impossible to tell which are
the rising and rapidly developing trades of the country ; changes are
much quicker in their operation than formerly, and self-equalisation may
be depended on more than in past times, owing to the facilities for
acquiring information, and for travelling from one part of the country to
another. Whatever supposed justification for such a course may have
existed in the past, or in particular trades, I am of opinion that the time
has certainly come for liberty of action in this matter. Now-a-days
events move so rapidly that some trades are frequently doubled or
trebled in the course of a year or two, and even some of the largest
trades in the country have been increased to an extent which it was
quite impossible to anticipate. A limitation of learners, which most
trades unions attempt, is in all such cases a direct injury to the community at large, interfering, as it does, with the extension of the general
prosperity of the nation. Besides, any attempt at monopoly in any
given trade is detrimental to the general interest of working men as a
class, and that which operates to the injury of the class as a whole will
eventually recoil on each individual. If certain skilled trades make
restrictions in their own favour, other branches suffer, and especially
those which are the worst paid of all, where little skill or knowledge is
required ; and it must also be borne in mind, that anything in the nature
of a fancy or unnatural wage, if maintained by such a monopoly, is a tax
on the general community. If it be urged, as it often is, that masters
would try to work apprentices so as to supersede skilled workmen, I
reply that it is impossible that this could be done with trades generally,
as the number of learners to do so could not be obtained, and if any
trades were found to be specially liable to such a course, nothing could
furnish a stronger proof that they were not entitled to rank as highly-
skilled, and they ought to take their proper place accordingly. The
rising generation must be absorbed in the labour market, and I think it
should be left free to avail itself of the best openings that occur, which

will no doubt be in the fast growing and best paying trades, where in the nature of things the least injury would be done to the older workmen. Under a free system some trades would absorb many more learners than they do now, without any one suffering, and, to the extent that they did so, other trades would be relieved. I now come to the consideration of the action of trades unions in regard to new and improved machinery. Whenever they oppose its introduction, or insist on the same rate of payment for work produced by it as for that produced by old and inferior machinery, I think they act against their own permanent interests ; commit injustice against the inventor and introducer of it, and also inflict a wrong upon general society. If wages are to be high, improved modes of production must be introduced. This is the only chance of keeping commodities so reasonable in price, as that trade may be maintained. If this principle be acted upon it by no means follows that high wages imply a dearness of production ; the cost of labour depending entirely on the amount of work done for a given sum of money, and not upon the sum total of the weekly wages of the workmen. In America, where labour is still dearer than in England, the American workmen, by the inventions which have been introduced for labour-saving processes, can send many articles to this country in which we have been apt to think we stood unrivalled, as, for instance, spades, shovels, axes, cooper's tools, and pumps. Also, in agriculture they have their gang ploughs, and drop the seed from them, and when the grain is ready the reaping machine is used, and the thrashing machine follows it. I say, then, that if wages are to be high, invention must have free scope, and to that end it is necessary that every one who introduces a better method of doing anything should derive an immediate advantage from it. We must also recognise the fact that the cheapening of any article is a direct boon to the public, and is in itself equal to a rise in wages to every consumer. It is time, then, that trades unions encouraged invention, looking beyond narrow, personal, and present interests of individuals to the general good and prosperity of all trades, and the welfare of the public at large. In this connection I should like to ask whether the opposition of the unions to piecework is wise. Should not greater diligence afford a just claim to higher wages ? Is it not a fact that in the past the English workman

has held is own, because he has done more work than his rivals, so that
if wages have been higher, the cost of labour has not been advanced
accordingly, and will it not in the end prove impossible for the English-
man to get higher wages than others, unless he does more work ?   I
think such action as practically leads to the paying of all hands alike, or
which sets a limit to the amount of work a man shall perform, is opposed
to the general interest.   I do not object to an average list price, or to an
average fixed wage, but I do to a hard and fast line.   Many conditions
may justify a deviation in the employer's favour, and yet be to the
advantage of the workman, such as better machinery, straightforward
work, without trouble or hinderance, and a guaranteed continuance of
work for a considerable length of time.   In such cases a written contract
should be entered into for a long period, and a guarantee given by the
employer to find full work or an equivalent in wages for the whole time.
This would not act, as some fear, to bring down wages in other than
those exceptional instances which justified a deviation.   Such a system
of working under agreement for a lengthened, definite, period, or subject
to a considerable notice either way, would be a great advantage, as
employers could not in bad times, by suddenly refusing to find work,
attempt to grind down wages ; the bonds between employer and employed
would be strengthened, and their interest would be more closely cemented.
Under such a plan the best men would do more work and get more pay,
which is sometimes held to be antagonistic to the general interests of the
workmen at large by making work scarce.   If this objection means anything, it means that it is desirable to encourage listless indifference
and careless idleness, and that mere drones should be supported by the
community at large.   My belief is, that piecework and a system of contract are essential to secure the interests of the general public, and that
they offer the best, if not the only, openings for the best men to rise.
How many have so risen—men of unbounded energy, ability, and enterprise, forcing their way from the ranks of those born to labour, becoming
the leaders in all great undertakings, and carrying, so to speak, the world
upon their shoulders.   In what other way can there be an incentive to
effort, or how can improvement be stimulated ?   It ought to be the
object of a workman's ambition to attain daily more subtle and exemplary
skill in his own craft ; he thus serves the world better, and ought to reap

corresponding advantages, so as to be able to save for his declining years, and to start his children in a better way. A gradual rise in social rank is thus possible to all well-conducted persons, and those of superior power and ability may rise to any height. Dead-levelism is antagonistic to the order of Providence. There should be constantly honest strife and noble effort. It is only by these that each man's proper place in the world can be determined. The question always is, and always ought to be, "Who is the best man?" no matter what for—for everything. "Every man as good as his neighbour," is the great social heresy of the present day. It is also a curse, and seems likely to prove one of the most withering, paralysing, and destructive curses the world ever saw. The workmen of England would raise the wildest howl of indignation if any one were to talk of going back to a system of protection in trade; yet all the while they are building up the narrowest and most ruinous system of protection around labour. Free trade means that each country shall have fair play to supply to any body that which it can supply best or cheapest. In like manner free labour would supply the best man for each post. "In all former slaveries, Egyptian, Saxon, and American, the slave's complaint has been of compulsory *work*. But the modern politico-economic slave is a new and far more injured species, condemned to compulsory *idleness* for fear he should spoil other people's trade." The chains are being daily wrapped more closely round the British workman and becoming more securely rivetted. Is there still left nerve and muscle and will enough to snap them? The manliness, the courage and determination —nay, even the honesty, of the masses of the English people, which have been our country's pride, are being crushed out of existence by so-called friends of the people, who say, "Stand up for your rights, get your division of profit—be sure you are as well off as others, and have what they have—are you not as good as anybody else?" A fair chance for every one will in the long run be found to be a far wiser policy than the repression of skill in favour of the unskilful, or in enforced idleness in the interest of the indolent. Our social economy would be all the better for a re-inoculation of a little of the spirit and sentiment which is implied in the old words, "He that will not work, neither shall he eat." I am not in favour of excessive work, without proper relaxation and rest. Work is holy, and rest is holy, and both are good for man; but idleness, which is neither rest nor work, is against the eternal laws of the Ruler of the universe, and in opposition to the interests of humanity. Another aspect of this same point must now be considered ; namely, the opinion held by many that the reduction of the hours of work, and the enforcement of higher wages, must of necessity improve the condition of workmen. If this could be done by a single trade, or a single locality, whilst it was not done by others, no doubt it would do so, but it would be a dishonest advantage taken of all the rest. Those who were guilty of it would be doing a less service *for* their fellow men than they were obtaining *from* them. An eminent writer, speaking on this point, says : " You have founded an entire science of political economy on what is stated to be the constant instinct of man—the desire to defraud his neighbour." The same principle applied universally, instead of leading to a better state of things, must necessarily lead to one much worse. If everybody does less work, the sum total of production is of a certainty reduced, and consequently each man's share must be less. Money is not wealth, and wealth is not money. Money is merely the machinery used for the transfer of wealth. It is a contrivance to do away with the cumbrous, old, barbarous system of barter. If everybody gets double the amount in money for what he produces, everyone will inevitably find that when he goes to market to spend his money he will only get half as much for it as it used to buy. Two Australian farmers might exchange corn and cattle on an agreement that for each head of cattle or each sack of corn an agreed number of marks should be made on a stone or notches cut in a tree, and they might keep their accounts straight. If one wanted to increase the number of marks he should put down for a given article the other would probably do the same, and what difference would it make ? None. Money is precisely the same thing as the marks, but adapted to more complicated transactions. If your neighbour digs an acre of land for you for 100 pennies, and you weave for him fifty yards of calico for the same number of pennies, of what advantage would it be to either of you to charge each other double the quantity of money for the same service. If one should wish to do this whilst the other did not, and could succeed in doing so, it would be an injustice, assuming that the previous arrangement was a fair one. Such an arrangement, however secured in the first instance, could not be permanently maintained. It would be an attempt to enrich oneself and to make another poor, and the poverty of others would recoil on ourselves. Service must be measured by service, and large wages can only be justified on the ground of large benefit conferred. "For one man to seek his own good at the expense of his neighbour's welfare has been, since dust was first made flesh, the curse of man ; and to do as you would be done by, the one source of all natural blessing." This is the Communism of the Father of us all, and His executive power is all sufficient to enforce His law. The question of what wages shall be given for a given quantity of work is often erroneously supposed to be simply a question between employers and employed as to the proportions in which profit shall be divided. The fact is not so. It is a question between the producer and the consumer. The employer's profit depends entirely on competition between rivals in business. What is paid for labour is simply an element in the cost, precisely the same in character as the cost of materials, the price of coal, or any other expenses. Temporary derangements and interference with profit may and will occur from fluctuations in any or all of these, even to the extent of loss of trade and a cessation of all profit. If these results be of long duration in any business, it will follow that as far as possible capital will be withdrawn and used in other ways. On the contrary, where profits are excessive more capital will be attracted, and competition increased until they are reduced. I have endeavoured to show that high wages ought not to be expected, otherwise than for efficient service rendered to the public, and that any attempt to obtain them on other grounds is an attempt to defraud society at large. I say just as emphatically the same of a manufacturer's or a merchant's profits. They can only be justified on the ground of legitimate service to mankind. Large profits obtained by unduly grinding down the wages of the employed, by untruthfulness, or by dishonesty to the public, I regard as the very worst kind of theft. No language can be too strong in condemnation of all deception and falsity in trade and commerce—falsity in workmanship, deception in quality or material, adulteration, and false measures and weights. "A false balance is an abomination to the Lord, but a just weight is His delight," and we find in the Levitical law this command, " Ye shall not steal, neither deal falsely, neither lie one to another."

Ruskin says, " No form of theft is so criminal as the making and selling bad goods—none so deadly to the State. If you break into a man's house and steal a hundred pounds worth of plate, he knows his loss, and there is an end ; besides, you take your risk of punishment for your gain like a man. But if you swindle me out of twenty shillings' worth of quality in each of a hundred bargains, I lose my hundred pounds all the same, and I get a hundred untrustworthy articles besides, which fail me and injure me in all manner of ways when I least expect it ; and you, having done your thieving basely, are corrupted by it to your heart's core. In such a crime there is added to the theft the baseness of its calculated betrayal of implicit trust, and the yet more perfect vileness of the obtaining such trust by misrepresentation, only that it may be betrayed; and this occult crime is blackened by the fact that it could not be committed at all, except by persons of good position and large know-ledge of the world. What is so wholly unpardonable, so inhuman, so contrary to every law and instinct which binds and animates society ?" It is said that " Fair play is a jewel," so is fair work, fair manufacture, and fair dealing. I am glad that laws are now-a-days being made with the view of dealing rigorously with all this kind of rascality, which is, alas ! so common that we can scarcely wonder at the poet exclaiming, " An honest man's the noblest work of God." I promised to speak of trades unions and federations of employers. Not having spoken of the latter, I will briefly do so. Combination, if of one side only, is liable to take a one-sided view, may over-run its purpose, and in the end defeat itself. I therefore recommend a mutual recognition of the rights of capital and labour, and of the identity of their interests ; more sympathy and a stronger bond of union between employers and employed, in place of the fatal jealousy of the past. If it is right that one side should combine, it is not less so that the other should. In fact, it seems not only just but necessary, that the power of organisation on one side should be met by organisation on the other. This by no means implies a state of warfare between the two classes. The defenceless state in which the want of organisation has left the employers of labour has tempted aggressive movements, which have operated largely to the injury of the public. In the interests of society in general, and to maintain the com-mercial prosperity of the country, it seems necessary that a balance of

power should be established, so that both should be compelled to listen
to the voice of reason. I in no way advocate war and conflict. All
that might be obtained by force on either side, ought to be peacefully
conceded if founded on justice. I have always advocated arbitration in
local disputes, and I can see no reason why the principle should not be
extended and more thoroughly organised. With trades unions on the
one hand and federations of employers on the other, each with power
sufficient to command the respect and consideration of the other, it
is probable, nay I think certain, that we shall eventually see developed
a national system of arbitration, with a representative National Council,
by which trade regulations should be endorsed, and to which local disputes might be referred when all other modes of settlement failed. All
sides of every question would be looked at ; the capitalists' side, the workmen's side, and the interests of the community at large. We should not
then read in the newspapers such paragraphs as the following :—"A mass
meeting of Ayrshire miners was held on Monday week, and after an address by Mr. Macdonald, M.P., it was resolved, on his advice, to restrict
the number of working days per week, and the number of working hours
per day, and thus by reducing the stocks of coal and iron, place a check
on the fall of prices and wages." Here no consideration is given to the
indisputable fact that the stocks have accumulated because extravagant
wages and prices have checked the demand, and so crippled the great
industries which consume large quantities of coal and iron, and on which
vast numbers of working men depend for bread. There is not a thought
given to the fact that, by such action, the men are not fighting their employers, but that they are plundering the community for their own
advantage, and committing an act of injustice which will be felt in every
cottage home in the land. Trades unions may and do commit errors,
and will be all the better for some counteracting influences. They are
sometimes one-side and one-eyed. On the whole, they have doubtless
been of immense value to the working classes, and I believe their benefits
will be much greater in the future, as with more enlightenment they will
become freed from the fallacies and errors of the past. But the true
beacon-light on which the working class should fix their constant gaze is
co-operation, the truest and the soundest solution of the difficulties which
surround the question of the rival claims and conflicting interests of

capital and labour. Co-operative land and building societies, co-operative stores, co-operative foundries, cotton mills, &c., have been conducted with great success, and to the full extent of their ability to do so. They are a perfectly legitimate and proper mode of competing with private enterprise for the profits of trade. In proportion to their success they will increase, and I see no reason why they should not in time attract large amounts of capital on the limited liability principle, and, to some extent, in the form of debentures with a fixed rate of interest. I must not omit to say a word or two on the important subject of taxation, and the proportions in which labour and capital should bear the burdens of the State. My opinion is that taxes should fall mainly on property and profits; such taxes seem honest and just; they meet necessity in the bravest and shortest way, and do not directly interfere with any commercial transaction. I have not much sympathy with indirect taxation on such articles of food and drink as are understood to be the common necessaries of the daily life of the working classes. They enter too directly into the cost of all production, and press heavily and unfairly on men with large families. But I cannot agree with the resolution passed at the recent Trades Union Congress at Sheffield, to the following effect :—"That the Congress is clearly of opinion that the Imperial revenues ought to be raised by direct levy on the annual value of realised property." This is open to the objection that those who save, including thrifty artisans, would be made to pay for those who are reckless enough to spend every fraction of their earnings. Everyone who enjoys the privileges of the State should be liable to the extent of his ability to pay his share of the cost, and a judicious system of indirect taxation on the articles which may be regarded more as luxuries than as necessaries is, I think, sound in principle. Taxing property and omitting to tax incomes is also open to the very grave objection that those who invested their profits abroad would entirely escape. I cannot extend this paper by speaking of such subjects as emigration, the Poor Laws, the Factory Acts, &c., although they fall within the scope of my subject in the most direct manner. Subjects also which have an indirect bearing on the question might be alluded to if we had time; everything, in fact, which concerns the elevation and advancement of the working classes — primary and technical education, science and art teaching, working men's clubs, cheap literature, and newspapers, &c. And it would not be out of place to speak of the importance of political power being in the hands of the people, whereby even-handed justice and equal chances can be secured for all. I will content myself with looking back on the struggles and the victories of the past with thankfulness, and forward to the future with hope. Much has been already done. Much remains to be accomplished. Under the new order of things mistakes will doubtless arise, but, with the universal spread of education and the consequent development of the intelligence of the masses, light will break through the darkness, and such a glorious day will dawn as has not yet been seen. Having been associated all my life with that political party which has fought with and for the people, I rejoice in the recognition of their claims by the other classes in the State, and have the fullest trust that, with the enlightenment of public opinion, the right results will come in the end, whoever may stand or fall. With the continuation of the blessings of peace in our own beloved land, which we have so long enjoyed, and avoiding anarchy by our love for the settled, but progressive, political institutions of our country, Old England will daily become more and more what it is our heart's desire it should be—the cherished home of a prosperous, a happy, and a free people. (Prolonged applause.)

C

FIRST NIGHT'S DISCUSSION.

Mr. W. A. RICHARDS said it was not until that evening he learned that he should have anything to say upon this question. Certainly it was not in his mind when he moved the adjournment of the debate, that he would be called upon to continue it ; and therefore, though the subject was one of such an important character, he felt he should not be able to say anything that was new. He would, nevertheless, endeavour to address a few remarks to those present on the question which was raised by Mr. Ward's paper, which he took to be the broad and general one of the relations of capital and labour, in their widest and fullest sense. Any one who brought a subject of such importance before his fellows was entitled to their warmest thanks, and he felt that they were under a deep obligation to Mr. Ward, apart from the labour he had bestowed upon his paper, for the opportunity he had afforded them of considering a question, to his mind, of more importance to the well-being of this country than any other. For until some foundation was established upon which the relations of capital and labour might rest with confidence that each would have its rights, both would be exposed to the warfare they had seen from time to time, and to the disastrous consequences which must follow. He thought no one would contend that any strike which ever took place — and this was the most aggressive form of conflict between capital and labour — conferred any real benefit on one side or the other ; for the injury done in the course of the strike, either to capital or labour, from whichever point the subject was looked at, always exceeded the gain which accrued. Mr. Ward, though he was entitled to their highest praise for the labour bestowed by him upon his paper, had, he thought, scarcely treated the subject as broadly as it was capable of being treated. It seemed to him that, generally, Mr.

Ward had only bestowed upon it that consideration which the system called political economy brought to bear in the matter. Political economy to him (the speaker) meant nothing more or less than that each should get as much as he could of what he wanted, so long as he could get it without absolute injury to his fellows. Such a system, therefore, appeared to him to be on all fours with the strife they were continually witnessing between capital and labour, and it did not appear to him that on any mere system of political economy could the just relations of capital and labour have their foundations. Mr. Ward told them that genius would always have its way, and that it would always have its value and get its price, which he took to be a form of illustration that he who had the most power would always have the greatest gains ; and yet Mr. Ward told them that capital was never to have excessive profits. The two things must surely seem conflicting. To him there did not appear to be any means of reconciling two such propositions ; for if he who had was to get all he might, and keep it, he could not have consideration for his fellows. He thought that much of the present relations of capital and labour was owing to the greed of capital in later years. In the present century capital had so monstrously asserted its demands, and had so pertinaciously insisted on those demands, that, to his mind, much of the present condition of society was owing to that. In the past to which he referred the sole aim and object had been, " How can I aggrandise myself ?" not, " How can I justly use what is put into my hands for myself and my fellow creatures ?" He thought that any consideration of this subject ought certainly to embrace the first principles of natural justice, and these did not seem to him to justify, generally, the principles of political economy, as he understood them—which really put into the form of a science the old couplet, that—

> He shall take who has the power,
> And he shall keep who can.

He believed that this was a doctrine essentially consistent with the principles of political economy, but utterly repugnant to all principles of natural justice ; and that it was only when masters and men practised what they preached that the relations of capital and labour would ever be brought into harmony. He knew that he was advocating a view inconsistent with all modern doctrines, but the view which he put forward had the advantage of a very great antiquity—an antiquity which certainly went further back than the Christian era, though it had in our Saviour its ablest exponent. He believed that we do not live only to make money, and that the end and aim of our existence was not merely the accumulation of riches ; and he believed that in proportion as we put out of sight the consideration which absorbed men's minds so much, to that extent would the interests of others be advanced and the happiness of all promoted. There was one branch of the subject upon which, if time had permitted, he had intended to say something—it was a vexed question —that of the Criminal Law Amendment Act, about which there was so much confusion of opinion, and which was adverted to by Mr. Ward in his paper. It was a subject, moreover, as to which he thought that accurate information would be of service to all. He had been able to express only in a general way his views on the matter before them, and he was afraid that they were views not very generally acceptable ; but he held the opinion that it could only be when men practised the doctrines they professed that these questions, which lay at the root of the prosperity of this country, would ever get their solution. (Loud applause.)

Mr. WILLIAM START, a working man, said he had listened very attentively to the paper read by Mr. Ward, and had carefully read it over. He had come to the conclusion that the paper was not especially levelled against the interests of labour. It must not, therefore, be understood that the whole burden of replying must rest upon the shoulders of the representatives of labour. Whilst there were some grave charges laid at the door of the representatives of labour, he believed that the charges laid at the door of the representatives of capital were of equal or greater weight. The sword of criticism was a two-edged one that cut both ways. They had many things to admit. They admitted that the bulk of working men were ignorant of the operations of the principles of political economy. The capitalist, in the past, had shown about an equal amount of knowledge, and labour had had as just a right for complaint as the capitalist. If capital and labour had each suffered injustices, the burden had especially fallen upon the shoulders of labour. They had to admit that working men and trades' unionists had occasionally made mistakes, but asked for an admission on the part of capitalists that they had not always proved infallible. So far, then, they stood upon the same platform, whilst mutually complimenting each other upon their faults. They admitted that capital, as well as labour, was necessary for the production of wealth. They were anxious to admit that capital and labour were necessary for the production of wealth. They were anxious to admit that capital and labour were identical in interest, but wanted to hold in their hand a just reason for the admission. Both were interested in producing wealth. Capital was interested in obtaining as much of the wealth as possible, and labour was interested in keeping as much of it as possible in their own hands. They did not object to capital taking its share of the wealth, but objected to it taking all the wealth, whilst it left labour a bare existence. " Unless a fairly just advantage be gained on both sides, the one will desert the other." Now, when there was a dispute between capital and labour, it happened generally that an advantage was sought on one side only, and they did not see how an advantage could be gained on both sides. It was rather that one side was called upon to surrender some of its advantages for the benefit of the other, that there may be a more equal distribution of wealth. They did not object to the accumulation of wealth, but objected to its accumulating all on one side. Let it be understood that they did not object to the "right"—"that the benefits arising from the joint action of capital and labour should be shared by both in the spirit of friendliness." " Many people appear to think that the capitalist is the natural enemy of the worker." In too many instances the capitalist had justified that manner of thinking by his grasping unfairness, by his iniquitous haste to get rich, and by the undue advantage he sought to gain over the worker. They had it laid down as conditions, that there shall be capital and there shall be labour. There must be capitalists and there must be labourers. As both were necessary for the production of wealth, both had rights and claims. Labour had to complain that capital had had all the consideration. Capital had had all the protection—all the legislation had been in the interest of capital—and labour, as one of the chief conditions of wealth, had been ignominiously overlooked. If capital was unfairly treated, it had the chance of deserting labour ; but if labour was unfairly treated, it had no chance of deserting capital. Labour had been helpless, and at the mercy of capital ; but labour was the source of all wealth, aided by former labour, or capital.   They had to complain that while combinations of capital and of capitalists had been encouraged and protected, combinations that directly represented labour had been ignored and treated as illegal, and were now regarded as highly dangerous.   Let it be remembered that the trades' unionist was interested as much in defending the interest of his trade, as the greatest capitalist in defending the interest of his capital.   (Hear, hear.)   And the trades' unionist was a man entitled to the respect of his fellow men ; for the fact that he was one, showed that he was thoughtful, and provident, and interested.   It was clear that classified labour was the most productive, hence the appropriation of trades or callings, which were once adjusted by law, but now by common consent (except in some few callings still privileged by protection of law).   As classified labour was necessary for successful production, and they were expected to bend their energies in some direction of classified labour, what was more natural than that they should require some security for the calling in which they had invested their interest and their lives ?   There were two sides to the question of security—the interests of labour required security as well as the interests of capital.   He was glad that Mr. Ward conceded the right of men to combine to further their common interest, although he found it difficult to draw the line of their justifiable action.   Mr. Ward had dealt some rather heavy blows upon the trades' unionist.   " He knows that individual liberty has often been trampled in the dust, and the most cruel coercion exercised, in the interest of trades' unions."   He had heard of them, and had no doubt that some of the statements had been greatly magnified ; but he could not say that he knew them from any personal experience.   He was not now a trades' unionist, but for the first eight or nine years of manhood he belonged to a very respectable, well-conducted trades' union, and, although he was young, rose to be the president of that society—namely, the Amalgamated Society of Engineers and Machinists.   To the honour of that society, he had never known a single act of coercive injustice practised by the society, or by individual members, although he had worked in shops where both unionists and non-unionists had worked together.   He was sorry that Mr. Ward did not see his way clear to " advocate the unconditional repeal of the Criminal Law Amendment Act."   The common law of assault ought to be sufficient for every emergency. (Hear, hear.) He was not disposed to justify every act of the trades' unions. They had no doubt made mistakes, and they were sorry for it ; but had the capitalists never made mistakes ? Had they never practised "rattening" of the deadliest character ? Had they no trades' unions, no Chambers of Commerce, no Chambers of Agriculture ? Had they not conspired against the interests of the labourer, and combined to crush the half-starved brute because he dared to ask to have one shilling added to his wages, and said he could not live and maintain himself and family on 13s. per week ? Not only were they rattened by the farmer and the squire, but were beset by noble lords and earls, who intimidated them by rabid, cruel speeches, and threats of extermination. Or they might be told by the brother of the Earl of Hardwicke that he had his eye upon them from London, and unless they accept the 13s. per week and withdraw from the union, they were in bodily danger ; and yet the Criminal Law Amendment Act failed to reach these noble intimidators. The Criminal Law Amendment Act was a blow levelled at the interests of labour, and was designed to favour the capitalist, and all the vaunted eloquence of the capitalist about individual liberty was a sham and a snare. The existence of the Criminal Law Amendment Act was a stigma upon the best of England's labourers. They knew Mr. Ward's argument upon this point, and were the more surprised that he should fail to see that the bases of English liberty rested upon equality before the law. Mr. Ward thought " that any action upon the part of trades to limit the number of apprentices, was unsound and unjust." Now it often happened that the action of employers was unsound and unjust also, and one injustice sometimes existed to counteract another. There were creatures in the shape of employers who had no consciences, who never study the interests of their workpeople or the public weal. The trade might be a limited one (it generally happened that any action of this kind took place in limited trades). The employer conceived a plan by which he might soon get rich. It was to work his concern by an unlimited number of apprentices, and this unlimited number of apprentices meant discharge to the workmen, or reduction of wages. Mr. Ward thought that, in the interests of free trade and free labour, the employer should be allowed liberty in this respect ; the trades think that the liberty of the employer here was their ruin. Here were supposed conflicting interests, and who should fix the standard of right? In this case, as in many others, might asserted the right. "A limitation of learners, which most trades' unions attempt, is, in all such cases, a direct injury to the community at large, interfering with the prosperity of the nation." He should like to ask Mr. Ward what class of men, other than working men, are called upon or expected to sacrifice the interests of their calling for the benefit of the community at large, or for the prosperity of the nation? This was never a consideration of the capitalist. If the town or the nation asked a favour of him, he sold it at a mighty dear rate. (Laughter.) Working men were pretty well lectured upon the virtue of resignation and large-heartedness, but they wanted to see some good examples in the other classes. If an employer created for himself a trade or a business, he tried to keep it to himself, and keep others from sharing it with him as long as he could. He patented his machinery and registered his patterns, for the purpose of keeping the trade to himself. The trades' unionist who, in this respect, protected his trade was an equal. With regard to trades' unionists fixing uniform wages, he thought that a mistake. He knew it was a mistake as far as his trade was concerned. What the trades' unions did was this :—like sick benefit and insurance societies, they tried to select the best men for their members, and the test of a man's goodness or ability was the amount of wages he received ; they therefore fixed a minimum price, or wage, at which they would accept members, and that minimum price was the average wage of the trade in the neighbourhood. The onus of uniformity of price rested with the employer. The employer thought he was wronged by the trade union fixing a price at all, and then said, " If you fix a price, I will pay no man above the price." The result was that, to meet the requirements of the better class of workmen, the price had to be raised, and the inferior workmen were dragged up in value, at the expense of the employer or the public. He was not aware that any trade society objected to any man receiving higher wages than the minimum, but the employer, if he was foolish enough, would refuse to give it. With regard to new and improved machinery, he thought the best and wisest workmen did not object to new and improved machinery. They had learnt better than to do so. But even on this head they had an objection to make, for it was found that improved machinery and improved appliances had been as strongly opposed by capitalists who had had vested interests in the old machinery, as by workmen. Stage coaches had objected to canals; and canals had objected to railways, and all parties had resisted just so far as a thing interfered with their immediate interests, and very few had had a sufficient amount of large-heartedness to cater for the public good. He was glad that the question of distribution formed a part of Mr. Ward's paper, and was included in the question of capital and labour. He was of opinion that we shall never be able to come to a right understanding on these matters, unless we include in them the question of distribution. As we are all interested in the production and accumulation of wealth, we are all interested in its distribution. The question of production was now pretty well understood, but the question of distribution was yet very complex. If you want to give an interest and a stimulus to production, you must give an interest in its distribution. There was no limit to our producing powers, but wisdom asked for a just system of distribution, which would make production more productive. There was something wrong in the social system which admitted of piles of wealth on the one hand, and poverty and wretchedness on the other. The social problem could not be said to be solved, whilst we have a million of paupers on the one hand, and a million of thieves and idlers on the other. The question of capital and labour was very imperfectly understood, whilst in this country thousands lack the necessaries of life, in sight of vast piles of wealth and plenty. Let the attention of the leading classes be turned in this direction for awhile, and they would be able to do something worthy of themselves. The vast masses born in this country were not asked whether they would be born, nor were they asked the conditions of their birth or station; all had a right to live, and to live well and happily, and there was no reason why it should not be so. The conditions of wealth were in the hands of this and of every civilised nation; they had mastered the necessity for poverty, and when they were wise poverty would have become a thing of the past. In conclusion, he should be blind if he could see no beauty in Mr. Ward's paper, in which there was food for thought for the capitalist and for the worker; and he thought Mr. Ward hit the right nail on the head when he dealt with co-operation as he had done. (Applause.)

Mr. T. H. FARMER proceeded to quote from the paper of Mr. Ward. Capitalists, even in Mr. Ward's sphere, could not work altogether alone on the precise amount of capital they possessed ; and then capital bore a certain elasticity. The trade of England, he affirmed, was much dependent on the principle of credit. Some time ago he read a paper to young men on the subject as to whether success in life was dependent on character ; and though much discussion took place constantly in reference to capital and labour, he maintained that the phrase capital and labour was not complete without the addition of the word credit, which, in itself, could only be obtained by character.

Mr. WARD remarked that "credit" simply meant using some one else's capital.

Mr. FARMER resumed, that there was great praise due to Mr. Ward for having read his very admirable paper. He said, "I must speak of trades' unions and federations of employers. So far as the object of trades' unions is to raise the working classes in the social scale, and on their behalf to resist oppression and injustice, my sympathy is entirely with them." It was very nice to hear of capitalists having sympathy with the working men. He also said, "Admitting freely that the rapacity, greed, and injustice of employers in many instances afforded a full justification for such a course as the adoption of a strike, I must now emphatically condemn many of the acts which have, in the past, been more or less associated with trades' unions." There was, no doubt, much force in all this, and he was satisfied that Mr. Ward's impulse in writing his paper had been one of the best of impulses. But why speak of "federations of employers," when simply referring to a union of employers ? In the same way it would be quite right to talk of trades' unions as "federations of workmen." As to himself, he might be allowed to remark that his pet subject was taxation. (A laugh.) Further, his paper on the subject had been deferred until next session, in consequence of the expected discussion on Mr. Ward's paper. That gentleman, he continued, said, "I must not omit a word or two on the important question of taxation, and the proportions in which capital and labour should bear the burdens of the State. My opinion is that taxes should fall mainly upon property and profits ; such taxes seem honest and just ; they meet necessity in the bravest and shortest way, and do not directly interfere with any commercial transaction." He must say that he did not feel quite in harmony with the whole of Mr. Ward's expressions. Mr. Farmer concluded by again adverting, in commendatory terms, to the paper before them for discussion. (Applause).

Mr. L. SIMONS said he was not present when Mr. Ward read his paper, but printed copies of it had been forwarded to him. He did not hesitate a moment to state that he agreed, for the most part, with the contents of the paper. He had read it with the greatest pleasure, and had found in it sound reasoning, good experience, and good advice, and he was very glad that the paper had been written, and that they were now discussing it. In these observations he did not wish merely to compliment Mr Ward. He wished to say a few words on the general contents of the paper, but in the first place he desired to refer to something of what they had heard from Mr. Start. For his own part, he had expected that trades' unions would have had a better idea about free trade. Mr. Start had said that when he was president of the local branch of the Society of Amalgamated Engineers and Machinists, a coercive measure was never carried out to his knowledge. But he (the speaker) recollected that a couple of years ago a union compelled his firm to pay so much more to every man, good or bad, with the alternative that otherwise they would go out. This he called coercive. (Hear hear.) Coming to the statments of Mr. Richards, he knew that Mr. Richards was a liberal man, and hoped that he himself had been so all his life. But in his remarks Mr. Richards would appear to be a real Communist — (laughter)—and might have done credit to the best in Paris two years ago. (Renewed laughter.) If the doctrines he had laid down were generally established in the world, he did not know that Mr. Richards would be allowed to live quietly in his residence, and to carry on his business as he did. (A laugh.) The title of Mr. Ward's paper was "Capital and Labour," against which nothing could be said, because the title was one generally given to this subject now before them, not only in English, but also in many other languages. Since national economy had grown into a science, the question of capital and labour had become of the greatest interest, though there was yet so much misunderstanding about it. He scarcely thought the title an adequate one. In his opinion, capital was not exactly that which should be put next to labour, for many possessed capital who did not know how to use it, in consequence of which a good deal of capital lay idle. He thought they should rather put it "Knowledge and Labour." There was a good old saying that "Knowledge was power." It was real knowledge which governed the world, and which had effected all the improvements that had taken place. Knowledge would create capital, but capital would never create knowledge. (Applause.) He asked how far the capitalist could occupy five or six hundred "hands," if he had not the brain that would enable him to do so? If they wanted a common expression, call it "brain and handwork." If a man made use of his time to learn, he would know more, earn more, and have a better chance of advancement. It would do away with much envy, hatred, and bitterness of feeling, if our workmen began to learn that in hindering the right use of knowledge, combined with capital, they did harm to themselves, and present experience should teach it to them. Frequently they had allowed themselves to be led by those who sought to gratify their ambition. If true knowledge would guide the men as well as the masters, it would be infinitely better for both ; and the probability was, that the result of this discussion would be to do good. (Applause.)

Mr. GEORGE ALLCROFT (Secretary of the Amalgamated Engineers) said that, as to the alleged coercion, he, being an officer of the Engineers' Society at the time it took place, and also at the present time, should possess a little knowledge which might throw light on the subject. He maintained that they should consider the reasonable expectations of a man who had served seven years to learn his trade. Then, he did not think a man should have to work merely for a bare subsistence ; he should be able to provide something against old age and sickness. It was, therefore, stipulated that the ordinary workman should have so much. Before a man could be admitted a member of the society to which he belonged, that man must be possessed of the requisite qualification. He had to be known by men working in his trade to be an ordinary workman, and the men who worked with him must surely be quite as good judges on this head as his employer.

As to any action they had taken, it must be recollected that there had been a diminution in the purchasing power of money. He maintained that the principle which he defended would bring up the unscrupulous employers face to face, and would have a desirable effect. The better class of workmen would always command a better rate of wages. In reference to that part of Mr. Ward's paper where he advocated the dividing of the funds of trade societies, it was a delusion for any one to think this would ever be instilled into the minds of the workmen. He proceeded, by references to statistics, to show the beneficent uses to which the funds of his own society were put. He thought it was right to fix an average rate of wages, for the best workmen would always command a better rate of remuneration than ordinary workmen. In his own trade this was so, and the same in others. As to piecework, he considered it the curse of every trade that had to do with it. (Applause.)

Mr. THORNLEY asked why it was that Mr. Allcroft should object to piecework ?

Mr. START remarked that it was not adapted to some trades.

Mr. S. HANCOCK said a gentleman at the other end of the room had remarked that in his trade they fixed a minimum rate of wages, but his own experience in the lace trade was to the contrary. He had known a twisthand to admit that plenty of men employed with him were not worth their salt. Why should an average be paid, if a man was not worth it ? If trades' unions would only classify their men, and be careful how they made an A 1 man, it would, he thought, be to their interest, and to that of all parties. (Hear, hear.) Their principle was one of dead-levelling, and led men to trust rather to being members of a union than to their own ability. (Applause.) If a society made the best of its members first-class men, this would be a recommendation to them up and down the country ; and a master, say in the cabinet trade, known to employ only first-class men, would command more money for his goods. He himself would be willing to pay more for goods made under such circumstances. He thought that the whole of this question required to be very carefully looked at : he maintained that the principle of dead-levelism was one of the greatest curses in trade unionism. A

man who was not a member of the union could not get into most of their
lace shops : if he was admitted all the men would strike, and thus the
employer was practically not master of his own concern. He should
like thoughtful workmen to take up that view of the matter which he
had endeavoured to set forth.   Mr. Start had made some allusion to the
Criminal Law Amendment Act, and he would perhaps be excused if he
referred to it.   He was satisfied that there was much misconception and
misrepresentation on the point, and much time might be saved by a clear
understanding of the subject.   Mr. Ward stated in his paper, " I unhesitatingly say that I believe it to be over-stringent in some respects,
and unjustifiable so far as it would touch acts when committed by trades'
unionists, which it could not reach if committed by other people. I do
not, however, advocate its unconditional repeal, without having something substituted in its place." He (the speaker) pleaded to having been
largely ignorant on the subject of this Act. He had gone through the Act
that day, and, to his surprise, there was not a word in it about trades'
unionists.   It had been said that under it the working man, if a trades'
unionist, was singled out, and that it was class legislation. Those who
passed the Act might have had trades' unions in their eye, but there was
nothing on the face of the Act which entitled it to the epithet of class
legislation. (Hear, hear.)   There might be one or two portions of the
Act which would come within the scope of Mr. Ward's remarks, but in
the main there was no difference between trades' unionists and non-
unionists. (Applause.)

  Mr. E. GRIPPER, after some observations on the subject of an
average rate of wages, said that if Mr. Start would permit him, he would
express the opinion that much of what that gentleman had said was
beside the mark.   He did not think any one would question that there
had been instances of hardship inflicted on the part of the employers, but
the assertion of facts such as these did not touch the question of the
position of capital as to labour.   He thought one great omission in Mr.
Start's reasoning was, that there seemed to be an assumption that there
were only the employed and the employers to be considered.   The interests of the outside public were apparently ignored. If Mr. Start would
look carefully through his argument, by the light of the knowledge and

conviction that there was a third class to consider, probably he would materially modify some of the statements he had brought forward. The subject of the position of the agricultural labourer did not meet the question, for the universal feeling throughout the country was that they had been badly used, and there was universal commiseration with them in the struggle which was going on. He must be allowed to express his astonishment at the arguments of his friend Mr. Richards. (Hear, hear, and laughter.) Before they broke up, however, as Mr. Ward could not now reply, he certainly wished to state his general approval of the line of argument adopted by him throughout his paper. This line of argument, he believed, would bear investigation—(applause)—and if they came to its consideration fairly, he believed that argument would receive very little modification. As to trades' unions, he himself deprecated the tendency to compel the better workmen to work down to their inferiors. (Applause.) Before sitting down he expressed the conviction that this discussion would tend to be satisfactory in its results. (Loud applause.)

SECOND NIGHT'S DISCUSSION.

(TUESDAY, APRIL 21, 1874.)

Mr. ALBERT RICHARDS (of the Moulders' Society) opened the adjourned discussion. At the outset he wished to say that he was exceedingly pleased at the action taken by the Literary Section of that Club, which, he considered, reflected the greatest credit upon the Committee, giving working men and trades' unionists, who had been so much attacked from time to time, the opportunity of defending themselves, and of expressing their views upon the great questions affecting the interests of labour. Though he was pleased to a great extent with Mr. Ward's admirable paper, he was not so much taken up with it as with the action adopted by the Literary Section of the Club. In the paper there was certainly a great amount of candour and truth, which did credit to the well-meaning and intelligence of Mr. Ward; yet, at the same time, he thought that gentleman laid himself open to being accused of the charge of unfairness—at all events, to some extent. It appeared to him that Mr. Ward attacked, or made too much to do about, the policy of trades' unionists, while he did not go sufficiently into the policy of the employers. If he felt called upon to make obvious what he termed "one-eyed notions and one-sided actions" on the part of trades' unionists, so, also, he should have dealt with the one-eyed notions and one-sided actions on the part of the employers. (Hear, hear.) Unionists and working men would admit that there had been a system of coercion and intimidation in many trades, and by many workmen; but there was not an intelligent working man in the country who would attempt to vindicate either coercion or intimidation. (Hear, hear.) If Mr. Ward had felt it to be right that he should point out these defects in connection with trades' unionists, he should likewise have told them, with respect to the employers, of such practices as "spotting" men, of the "black list," and the character system, all of which were a disgrace to the civilization of the country. (Applause.) While there were employers who would scorn to do a mean action, or take a paltry advantage of their workmen, there were others who would not scruple to do so ; but that this was so they had no right to blame employers generally, nor should Mr. Ward do anything of the kind with respect to the working classes. Mr. Simons's remarks upon handwork, or labour, and intelligence seemed to him an insult to the common sense of working men. (Cheers.) Intelligence and know-ledge were not always associated with capital, and Mr. Simons should certainly have qualified what he said. Mr. Hancock's observations upon the subject of the Criminal Law Amendment Act were altogether beside the mark. He and his fellow workmen assembled there believed the idea of the Committee was to see whether nothing could be done to draw the relationship of capital and labour more closely together. (Hear, hear.) He was pleased with what Mr. Ward said on the subject of co-operation, which he considered to be a proper principle ; and he should like to see some of the employers of labour in Nottingham and through-out the country emulating the example of some other employers of labour. He himself used to work for one Mr. Gimson, at Leicester, who had taken all his men into partnership with him, giving them an interest in his business. If he still worked in that business he should work all the harder for the adoption of the plan—he would do as much work as he could, and would do it as well as he could, for by so doing he should benefit both himself and his employer. But some might disagree with this kind of partnership. They were speaking on this question of co-operation the other night at the Nottingham Cobden Club, when an employer asked, "Supposing, at the end of the year, there was a loss of £200 or £300 on the concern, or perhaps a loss of £1,000, what then ?" Why, as sensible men, if they participated in the profits they would expect to share in the loss. He had been gratified to hear the observa-tions made by Mr. W. A. Richards, which did infinite credit to his head and heart ; and he thought many speakers had misrepresented what he had said. Because the speaker to whom he referred said that in the distribution of wealth, or in the consideration of the question, the prin-ciples of natural justice should be regarded, he asked, did it follow that the speaker was a fit subject for the Commune, or was a Communist ?

D

(Hear, hear.)   He himself was not a Communist, though he might perhaps be accused of it if he tried to follow out the arguments of that speaker.   He recollected that in the *Spectator*, in November, 1872, a list of millionaires and wealthy capitalists was given, who had died during the preceding ten years.   Each of these had, on the average, accumulated no less a sum than £250,000 personalty.   They could imagine the amount of superfluous wealth possessed by these lucky individuals.   With such facts before them, they could understand how it was that England was the richest country in the world—that was, the rich were more numerous in England, according to the numbers of the population, than in any other country in the world.   Yet they could scarcely understand how it was that, at the same time, England was the poorest country in the world — that was, there were more people in it who were paupers, and on the verge of pauperism, than in any other civilized country.   They could account for the influx of wealth into the country, by the introduction of chemical and mechanical science, as applied to manufactures ; and they could also understand that it was the monopoly of these sources of wealth in the hands of a comparative few, that made our capitalists millionaires and our working men paupers. (Hear, hear.)   Towards the close of the last century a few important inventions gave birth to our gigantic factory system.   Capitalists stepped in, and rapidly became possessed of enormous fortunes.   But how did the workmen fare ?   What might be termed small partnerships were injured, the huge machinery of the factory destroyed the limited contrivance and humble inventions of the cottage, and as workmen were superseded by machinery pauperism was extended. Associated action on the part of working men might have benefited them under the circumstances, but the law stepped in to prevent it.   Trades' unions and co-operative societies have done much for the men.   Associated action on the part of workmen was made criminal, and workmen dare not combine for fear of imprisonment.   The result of all this was, that the wealth of the country flowed copiously into the coffers of the few, while the hardworking portion of the population could not share in that wealth.   (Hear, hear.)   Their ingenious men invented machines, and their industrious men worked them ; there was, however, no thought for equity in distribution, and the consequence was then, as now, more than enough on the one hand, with hunger and want on the other. Those individuals referred to in the *Spectator*, as mentioned, left no less than £60,000,000 sterling personalty, and during the same ten years there was so large a number of paupers. It was surely of importance, then, to take to heart the relationship existing between capital and labour. It was making no attack on property to say that the present comparison between excessive wealth on the one hand, and extreme poverty on the other, was a disgrace to England's boasted Christianity and her vaunted civilization. (Loud applause.) It might be very well for the few, who displayed their grandeur before the toiling masses of the people who were hungry; but, nevertheless, it was a disgrace, and he would say dangerous. (Hear, hear.) In our agricultural districts, and in our towns and cities, we have men with families who cannot find them the necessaries of life. Mr. Ward said that "to make England happy, men must feel that they have an interest in the country;" but what interest had working men in the country when thousands of them were in such a condition? He was touched the other day in reading the *Agricultural Labourers' Chronicle*, where Joseph Arch mentioned a poor agricultural labourer, with nine in the family, who, in the act of getting his scanty meal, offered up the prayer:

> Oh, Heavenly Father, help us,
> And keep us all alive;
> Around the table nine of us,
> And only food for five.

As to an illustration given by Mr. Ward, he contended that no man had a moral right to possess millions of cakes when thousands of hungry stomachs were wanting them. He might speak of the question of the limitation of apprentices, or of that of new and improved machinery, or on the apprentice question generally; but he did not intend to do so, for he was anxious that the rest of his fellow working men should have an opportunity of expressing themselves, and as others were going to take up different points, he thought it would be better for him, personally, to speak of capital and labour, or wealth and poverty, as a broad question. But he must say a word in reference to the remarks on the Criminal Law Amendment Act by Mr. Hancock. That gentleman said something to the effect that a man could not be put in prison, under that Act, for the distribution of tracts. He hoped to be able to prove that Mr. Hancock was in the wrong, for he had a list of prosecutions there had been under the Act. There was one John Turk, connected with a strike at Newcastle, who, for distributing handbills on the highway, was ordered off by a policeman. The man still stopping, was put into prison, and three days before his trial had to submit to all the indignities of a common felon ; and the punishment inflicted on him in connection with his trade, could not have been inflicted upon an ordinary citizen under the ordinary law. He should like to speak as to the Royal Commission, for he was rather surprised at Mr. Ward on this head. That gentleman spoke about " Her Majesty being graciously pleased to appoint a Royal Commission" on the subject of the laws affecting labour ; but he (the speaker) did not approve of the appointment of the Commission. He maintained that the time was already ripe for alterations in the matter ; but he would now, however, conclude, for there was an old Scotch proverb, " Blessed is the man that maketh a short speech, for he shall be invited to speak again."   (Laughter and applause.)

Mr. J. W. DOUSE said he should not have obtruded his thoughts on the meeting, but from the fact that he was one of a large class who for various reasons were non-unionists, and coupled with this he felt that for justice to be done to this deeply absorbing and important subject, it was absolutely necessary that the thoughts of a class of men generally ignored by unionists altogether should, in a discussion of this class, show that they had a stake or interest in the common weal. He should best serve his purpose by at once declaring that generally he was in accord with the writer of the paper, which was unique in itself, and ought to be possessed by every workman. It would bear reading more than once, and contained food of a most wholesome and salutary kind, that appealed at once to the thought, the reason, and the judgment of both capitalists and workmen. (Hear, hear.)   A quaint writer once observed, that however keen a man's appetite, " He eats, and lo ! 'tis gone."   But in this paper the theme was so skilfully handled, that the deeper we dive into it, we still have deeper depths to sound. He could not refrain from thanking Mr. Ward for what he had done, and the paper being cast on the waters of public criticism, he hoped its fruit would be seen after many days. He did not agree with Mr. Simons, that it would be better to substitute the word knowledge for capital. They were agreed that capital and labour had each its distinctive duties, and the neglect of the duty of either must endanger the happy relations that should exist between employer and employed. The primary duty of both was to frankly acknowledge the most perfect freedom of both. The men must be free, and the masters also ; and the joint rights of both must be built on security of property. If the rights of either were violated, then production and distribution would be languishing, or partially suspended. These and kindred thoughts compelled him to ask, was it right to limit the freedom all claimed as a birthright ? Freedom in a sense had it is limits, but it was convenient to inquire, are the actions of trades' unions, in curtailing individual freedom, carried beyond or kept within those limits ? If unionists asked when they curtail the freedom of the man, he answered that the ways were legion, but one instance would suffice, and that was touched on by Mr. Ward in what was called the *minimum* of wages, which emphatically declared that a man should receive a sum named by the union, say 30s. a week, and must not work for a less sum. It often happened that some one felt he was not a first-class workman—not so competent as others—but they virtually told that man that although he could obtain constant employment at 25s., he must not take it. The consequence was, he was always changing, no master being willing to pay 30s. for him when he was not worth it ; and perhaps half his time would be unemployed. In such a case the unions would rather, he believed, pay that man to walk the streets than he should work for less than was endorsed by the union. This was an injustice to the man, a malappropriation of the union's funds, and a tax on the consumer. These cases might be enlarged upon, but he passed onwards. The great error of the unions seemed to him to be the utter exclusion of public rights to the agrandisement by each of their own particular order. This error seemed fraught with extreme danger, and if carried to its logical conclusion must be subversive of morality itself. To live and let live was a trite but Christian axiom, though it seemed doomed. The crisis of the colliers he considered an illustration. During the last two years their action had stultified trade, brought no appreciable benefit to themselves, and had placed on the verge of ruin hundreds of honest traders, besides depriving millions of one of the prime necessaries of life. (Hear, hear.) But, further, take the case cited by Mr. Ward, wherein an M.P. lent himself to such advice as that given to the miners in Scotland. This case was at least one that ranked amongst the injudicious. Another phase was seen in the leaders of several unions stigmatising a certain M.P. for sitting on a Commission to which they were nominated, and advising all unionists to refuse to give evidence. In fine, it appeared to him that an amount of selfishness was being engendered that compelled a thinking man to pause ere he subscribed to a code of rules which dethroned individual freedom, made the word free trade a paradox, and subverted that golden rule which ought to be indelibly engraved on the hearts of all civilised people, "To others do as you would have others do to you." With respect to the Criminal Law Amendment Act, he thought of hearing some sound argument from Mr. Start in favour of its repeal, but Mr. Start failed to show any cause why. Declamation was not argument, neither was the calling in question of the design of our legislators, or the honesty of their intentions. (Hear, hear.) At least, these things did not convince him. He fancied in more than one place Mr. Start might have been consistently reminded that two blacks did not make one white. (Applause.) But he (the speaker) inclined to the opinion that that law required supplementing so as to reach employer as well as employed. (Hear hear.) He contended that it was applicable to both non-unionists and unionists, but frankly admitted it had been unduly strained in several cases, by both the paid and unpaid magistracy. (Hear, hear.) Let it not be thought that he advocated the abolition of the unions of the men—far otherwise. He saw in them, when properly used and judiciously conducted, a mighty lever calculated to raise labour from the slough of degradation, and to place workmen in an atmosphere so rarified that every vestige of slavery would soon meet its deserts, eternal banishment ; and then with the royal stamp of freedom on the workman's brow, none should cringe before capital or go in fear of molestation by their fellows, and every unit that went to make up the aggregate of labour, should represent a blossom in the glorious tree of universal liberty. That life-giving and peace-preserving tree had been threatened, but his soul still echoed the old, old lines—

> Woodman spare that tree,
> Touch not a single bough,
> In youth it shelter'd me,
> And I'll protect it now.

(Applause.) He was of opinion that the separation of the funds, as adverted to by Mr. Ward, was a reasonable proposition, and worthy the attention of leaders of the unions. He did not think Mr. Allcroft seemed disposed to give it that amount of consideration it deserved. He was of opinion that the limiting of apprentices was an evil, and no real safeguard to the aggregate of labour. He believed a hard and fast line would ever prove an apple of discord, and heartily concurred with Mr. Ward that the finest lever they could safely use to justly remedy the ills of life was to be found in the principle of co-operation. (Hear, hear.) He would urge his fellow working men, and the employers too, to cultivate a feeling of trust in each other. Let them do their work as they would wish to have it done if they were employers. Let employers, also, be considerate and give with no niggard hand, without undue pressure, what justice demanded ; and let them never lose sight of the noblest way to settle disputes, should they arise, namely—arbitration. In the interests of their children and coming generations, let them never neglect a sound and healthy education. Then would the millions of paupers and criminals gradually disappear. Then would those jealous feelings between the classes cease to exist, and each, whatever his station, would perceive it a duty to hand down intact to posterity, e'en as we prize them ourselves, the heaven-implanted principles of love and liberty. (Cheers.)

Mr. MATTHIAS MATHER said it might be that he would not occupy much of the time of his hearers, and that he would not be able to amuse them with his remarks, as the last speaker had done, who was not a member of a trades' union ; but, as a workman, he would endeavour to speak as closely as possible to the paper written by Mr. Ward, in which there was a good deal he could endorse. With Mr. Albert Richards, he thanked Mr. Ward for the many benefits working men had received from his determined support of the educational movement in Nottingham, and he was not at all disposed to underrate either Mr. Ward's abilities or intentions. It was not his wish to defend the abuses of trades' unions, or to maintain infallibility on their behalf. If trades' unions were not infallible, their opponents pointed triumphantly to their errors ; but infallibility could not be expected on the part of trades' unions, any more than on the part of employers. Perfection could not be expected from man. In the first part of the paper to which he would refer, Mr. Ward said, "There is a feeling abroad of bitter antagonism between the two, and many people appear to think that the capitalist is the natural enemy of the worker." He thought so, but he did not accept Mr. Ward's definition of capital—namely, that capital was accumulated labour ; for if he did, he should wonder how it was that accumulated labour was not in the hands of those who laboured to produce it. (Hear, hear.) Capital should be divided under three heads : land, accumulated labour, and money—the latter being an equivalent and representative of both the former. When he said that he believed capital was the natural enemy of the worker, he alluded to the capital of the aristocratic and landed classes, which was used rather for destruction than production ; for by the accumulation of vast estates into few men's hands, they were enabled to let or cultivate one-half, whilst the other half produced nothing but game, paupers, and criminals. The former devoured part of the produce of the cultivated lands, while the latter devoured the vitals of our civilization. So far as the force of supply and demand could operate, they obtained the same amount of money, in shape of rent, for the half that was in the market as though the whole were in useful occupation. And all that capital, which was not accumulated labour in its virgin state, nor in its present state so far as its owners were concerned, made them hereditary legislators, thus giving them equal legal power with the whole of the nation. It also made them county magistrates, so that they were not only national rulers, but often local despots. But he would return more closely to the subject of the paper, in which was a a passage of a somewhat simple character—the illustration as to Mr. Ruskin and his cake. Mr. Ward said the point of which he was speaking was put very clearly by Mr. Ruskin, who stated, "If a man does not eat his cake to-day, he ought to be allowed to have it, without grudging, to-morrow." The fact of a man having a cake for yesterday, gave him no right to it whatever. The question was, whether or not he had come to it by honourable and just means. (Hear, hear.) Suppose the capitalist, with money, said to the workman, who had only his labour, "If you will bake me six cakes, you shall have one." That being done, supposing each ate a cake to-day, the capitalist would have four left to-morrow and the labourer none. Could the labourer not begrudge the possession of those four cakes? (Hear, hear.) Then, still quoting from Ruskin, "If a man works for a thing, he shall be allowed to get it, to keep it, and to consume it in peace." That was what a trade's union did. As to its being said that capital, pure and simple, obtained a less rate of interest in England than elsewhere, the statement was correct, so far as concerned loan capital, but not quite so true when applied to capital employed in trade ; that they knew by the profits obtained in their co-operative establishments. Mr. Ward said, "The forethought and enterprise which lead to sound speculation as to the future neces- sities of the public, may all yield large profits without the slightest injustice to the labour employed." Yes, perhaps to the individual labourer employed. But if it was true, as stated by Mr. Ward, that wages were an item in the cost of production, and charged to the public, then it was true that profits were also an item, and charged to the public ; and whatever injustice there was in the one, there was surely the same in the other. Next, "I must emphatically condemn many of the acts which have been in the past more or less associated with trades' unions." But let them inquire how far these acts were associated with unions. He admitted they were trade outrages, but not that they were trades' union outrages, as stated. If they belonged to trades' unions in this manner, surely it would be true that the most mighty union would also have the greatest number of such acts in connection with it ; yet those unions which had great funds and great numbers of members, had scarcely been found to have been guilty of any kind of outrage, while those societies in in Sheffield which were found guilty of those acts were among the weakest and meanest in the country. (Hear, hear.) When men felt themselves aggrieved, if they had funds and means to secure redress of their grievances, they were not prompted by their animal passions to resort to violence, as was the case with men who were not so placed. Thus the weakest societies had always been found guilty of the most outrage ; and in the discussion on the Trades' Union Bill, Mr. Bruce said he had been in a certain district where there was no union at all, but where every species of outrage was perpetrated. (Hear, hear.) Similar testimony was to be found in the evidence given before the Trades' Union Commission. The acts of which Mr. Ward complained were, therefore, evils resulting from the state of society, and not the result of unions. (Applause.) That gentleman said, "I know perfectly well that I am now on delicate ground. Nothing is more debateable, and, in fact, nothing is more keenly discussed now-a-days, than the laws which have been directed against these very abuses." He must again beg to differ from Mr. Ward, for if the laws had been directed against the abuses, they would have been directed against any person committing them, whereas they were levelled at the unionist only ; for if he was a "black sheep" he might laugh at a unionist and the law would see no harm in it, but if a unionist laughed at him, the law would discover molestation. As to the last speaker being isolated by trades' unions, he had rather isolated them by not being a member of one. (Laughter.) Then, "I know that individual liberty has often been trampled in the dust, and the most cruel coercion exercised, in the interests of trades' unions." He (Mr. Mather) also knew that individual liberty had often been trampled in the dust, and the most cruel outrage and coercion exercised, in the interests of the capitalists. (Applause.) He would give them an instance, the accuracy of which he could vouch for, which would show the manner some of the employers adopted to carry out their plans. A few weeks ago five men left their employment because they thought proper to do so. Their late employers sent letters round to the various shops, requesting others not to employ them, in conformity with one of the rules of the Masters' Association. The result was, the men did not get employment—(cries of "Shame")—and in all probability some of these letters would find their way into the hands of the Royal Commission. In reference to arbitration, he would help Mr. Ward all he could to do away with the infernal system of striking—for he could characterise the system by no other term. He noticed, however, the failures which the Amalgamated Engineers had encountered by trying arbitration in Nottingham. They had tried arbitration twice, and failed both times—on the first occasion in consequence of not being able to agree, for which no one was to blame, either on the part of the workmen or employers. On the second occasion, three workmen, members of the before-mentioned Society, met three employers, representatives of the Masters' Association, and after about two hours' discussion of a very kindly character, they settled the dispute to the satisfaction of all present. The represensentatives of the Amalgamated Engineers' Society returned to their fellow-workmen, read them the agreement drawn up and signed by the arbitrators, and bade them present themselves at work next morning. The men did so, but the employer had altered the conditions agreed to by the arbitrators, and would not have them except on his own terms. The men refused to commence work, except on the decision of the arbitrators ; and the employer forthwith published a list with thirty-five names on it, calling upon the trade not to employ them. That was no secret, for the cards were shown to the men, and many of them had them. Now not only did the employers of the trade, with one exception, refuse to employ them, but the very arbitrators who had represented the masters also refused. He (the speaker) went to one of the arbitrators personally and said, " Will you not employ one of these men, who offers to return to work on your own agreement ?" and he said, " No, not until his late employer sends me word that he has done with him." Now it was not to be supposed that all those men were blackguards, for they were nothing of the kind, one of them occupying an eminent public position. That did not show that arbitration was at fault—it only showed that while they trusted to arbitration, they must not neglect their union. As to the limitation of apprentices, though a trades' unionist and treading on delicate ground, he did not think the limitation as at present carried on was wise or just, though not from the same reasons as urged by Mr. Ward. That gentleman said, " Because it is imposssble to tell which are the rising and rapidly developing trades of the country." It was also impossible for employers to tell which were the rapidly decreasing trades of the country. He (Mr. Mather) objected to the limitatation of apprentices because it was one person dictating the destiny of another, which, he held, no person had a right to do, unless he had forfeited his liberty according to the laws of his country. He contended that any child had a perfect right to learn any legitimate business it had the ability to learn, without let or hindrance from any person ; for learn he would some trade or other, and the consequence was that those trades which did not place any restriction upon the number of learners became swamped with them, while the trades that limited them obtained

unnatural advantages at the expense of those who did not. He could
think of nothing more selfish than for a man to exclude his own son from
his own trade, and then send him to learn the trade of another. If it
came from choice, or that his own was not good enough, then he did not
blame him ; but if it was for self-aggrandisement, it was a cowardly
wrong. That was a question the settlement of which should not be left
to what had been called the absolute liberty of the individual, irrespective of who that individual might be ; neither would he allow any employer to take all he could get. There ought to be a council composed
of workmen and employers, whose business it should be to say to what
shop the person applying should go to learn. They should not interfere
as to whether he should learn the trade or not, the choice being left to
the applicant. He would adopt that plan to prevent any avaricious
employer from working sudden evils by overstocking with boys. With
regard to its being impossible to supersede skilled workmen by
apprentices, it was not impossible in some trades. Mr. Nasmyth
said that by machinery and apprentices he reduced his workmen one-
half, that his profits were largely increased, and that he considered
it beneficial that there should be more men seeking employment
than there is employment to give. (*Vide* Report Royal Commission,
1867 and 1868, ques. 19,137, 19,139, and 19,145.) As to the
opposition of workmen in any instance to new and improved machinery
being against their own interests, an injustice to the inventor and introducer of it, and calculated to inflict a wrong upon society in general,
he would say that if the workman was always to make room for improved
machinery, it appeared to him that as machinery became developed men
must move off, and that the world was for machinery, not men. (Laughter and applause.) Nevertheless, he did not believe that the inventor
had reason to complain of the action of trades' unions, and he was inclined to think the capitalist as great an enemy to the inventor as any
class. For instance, the capitalists had always been the law makers.
They had gone to Parliament, and enacted such patent laws in this
country that absolutely prohibited the poor inventor from securing the
results of his own genius. What must such an inventor do ? Unfold
the whole secret of his invention to some capitalist, to induce him to pay
for the patent, in order that he (the inventor) might get at most a share,

when, if he was lucky, his name would be second in the business, and he be bidden to be thankful for the crumbs that fell from the rich man's table. As reference was made to the introduction of inventions in America, he observed that it was because there any one with brains making a discovery could obtain a patent for a very small fee indeed ; and then he could go forth to sell his patent, if he had not the means to work it himself. He might show it to as many and refuse as many as he pleased, without any risk of its being pirated. Those were the reasons why America was superseding them with her inventions. With respect to piecework, he objected to it, having seen its evil effects, and while the employer was not responsible for the wages of a man while in the work-shop, he would oppose it. (Hear, hear.) He had seen too much of setting two men to do the work of one, in order to drive the better bargain with either, thus profiting by the natural, and consequently barbarous, force acting between supply and demand—a force that, while it acted with redoubled cruelty towards the worker, played very mildly with the capitalist. For instance, when the worker took advantage of it, it was always when his employer and the trade generally were in pros-perity; but when the capitalist took advantage of it, it was always when the worker was at the poorest. But he did not blame any one for this, it was the inevitable result of circumstances—viz., individualism. Mr. Ward said, " Is it not a fact that in the past the English workman has held his own, because he has done more work than his rivals ?" Now, if that be true, why not give him the credit ? It should not be forgotten that that had been done in a country where trades' unions had been most powerful and universal. That sounded curiously contradictory, coming from the lips of a gentleman who said that trades' unions were paralyzing the industries of the country. As to its being asserted that the most skilled trades obtained the best pay, if they looked throughout the country they would find the amount of wages received by men rather in proportion to the strength of their unions. Though himself a mechanic, he did not believe that the disparity between the skill of the mechanic and that of the agricultural labourer, warranted the former in obtaining three times as much as the latter. (Applause.) Mr. Ward said, " And will it not in the end prove impossible for Englishmen to get higher wages than others, unless they do more work ?" His answer to that was, No, because they had natural advantages that others had not. For instance, they had geographic advantages, they had also geologic and climatic, all of which the meanest person in the country had a natural right to. He now came to the assertions respecting average wages, dead-levelism, and minimum. It must be apparent to all that it was an absurdity to say that any trade insisted on the average wages being paid to all. The average being the mean between two extremes, proved that some got more and some less. Many of the speakers had used the words average and minimum as though they were synonymous ; and all those who had spoken on behalf of capital had asserted, time after time, that a minimum wage system meant a dead-level, but not one of them had attempted to show by any argument that such was the case He was not aware of any trade that insisted on paying all men alike, nor ever did, except when the masters (for such they were then) had the power ; they fixed a maximum rate of wages, and the level was a dead one indeed. Mr. Douse asserted that trades' unions compelled an employer to pay more for some men than they were worth—that they obliged him to pay 30s. when the man might not be worth more than 25s. He (the speaker) would explain what was meant by the minimum rate of wages among trades' unionists. It was the lowest wage at which the union would admit them as members, and when they were admitted they said they would not work for less. A man was valued before he could join the society of which he (the speaker) was a member. He must, first, have worked five years at the trade, to ensure that he had had some time for practice ; the employer for whom he then worked (of his own free will, without any interference from the society,) must have paid him the minimum rate of wages, thus giving them the master's valuation of him ; after that, the men who worked with him, and were members of the society, must say that they thought he was worth what his employer was paying him. The next passage in the paper to which he would refer contained the old maxim, "He that will not work, neither shall he eat." He heartily wished, with Mr. Ward, that such a state of society could be brought about ; and when it was, he had every reason to believe that fustian would get as good a dinner as broadcloth. In reference to Mr. Ward's remarks upon the shortening of the hours of labour, he begged to say that although he got no more food or clothing for his extra money, he still got the same, and worked so many hours per week less. Mr. Ward illustrated that in another way. He said, "If your neighbour digs an acre of ground for you for one hundred pence, and you weave for him fifty yards of calico for the same money, what advantage would it be to either if you charge each other double for the same service?" Most certainly none ; but Mr. Ward would please observe there was no capitalist in the question. If a third party would step in as middle-man, or profit-taker, and take twenty-five per cent. out of each man's earnings, then it would matter whether the middle-man had it or himself. Mr. Ward said, "What is paid for labour is simply an element in the cost of production, precisely the same in character as the cost of materials, the price of coal, or any other expenses." Just so to the capitalist, but not to the labourer ; for it was a mistake to suppose that labour was anything *per se*, as it could not exist apart from the man. He could not save his labour from day to day, or send it from market to market. As to co-operation, he believed, with Mr. Ward, that it was the only true solution of the difficult problem they had before them. He was waiting anxiously for the time when unions should cease to be necessary, but he believed that as long as the present condition of things existed they would be necessary. (Hear, hear.) He approved of co-operation, which was for a person to employ his own capital and be employed by it. It was such an extensive subject, however, that he would content himself, in sitting down, by saying that he endorsed nearly all Mr. Ward had said as to the subject of taxation. (Loud applause.)

Mr. THOMAS HILL said that now they had heard three workmen speak, he wished to be allowed to offer a few observations. He did not himself think that trades' unions were of that great benefit which some people conceived them to be. It occurred to him that there was one class of workpeople in this country, whose wages had advanced in a higher ratio than any other class had experienced, and there was no union connected with this advance. He referred to domestic servants. (Hear, hear.) The first speaker, he thought, seemed rather as if he was angry. (Laughter.) However, there had been much said in the course of the discussion, but he did not think anything had been advanced as to how the present state of things should be remedied. He deprecated any impression that capital and labour were two contending armies, and maintained that they were brothers in one family, which family was the nation. (Hear, hear.) As to excessive fortunes, some would be able to remember trades springing up in their lifetime, and those who had seen the way to their management had made fortunes. As to labour being able to participate more than it did in the profits of capital, he was of opinion that they could not do it. With respect to co-operation, there was a co-operative business established in this district some two or three years ago, about which he should be glad to hear something. The freer they could have trade the better. He viewed with disfavour anything like caste among the working classes. He asked, were those at the top of the tree the sons of gentle people or not? What was Brassey, George Stephenson, or Arkwright? (Hear, hear.) Those who would fetter and bind business did not look into the matter very deeply, as to do all this was very unsound. He should like some one to speak of the way in which they would rob the capitalist and get his cake. (Laughter.) As to advances of wages, if all were raised alike no one could be benefited, and people were not a bit better off when a penny was worth sevenpence. The raising of the wages of the agricultural labourers would mean that the price of bread, and meat, and vegetables would be raised. (" No.") There could be no doubt, however, that if five trades out of fifty were raised, those five trades would be benefited, and this might be taken as a principle. (Applause.)

Mr. CHATWIN (President of the Amalgamated Society of Joiners) said he must first be allowed, on his own behalf and on behalf of the Amalgamated Carpenters and Joiners, to thank Mr. Ward for bringing this matter forward, also, to thank the Committee of the Literary Section of the Nottingham Liberal Club for inviting discussion on the subject, as he thought the fairest way to come to a right conclusion was to hear both sides of the question. He hoped that when this matter had been fully discussed, both employer and employed would have derived an advantage therefrom. (Hear, hear.) Mr. Ward said, "No lengthened injustice can exist on either side without those who sow the wind reaping the whirlwind." He contended that a very lengthened injustice had existed on the employers' side of the question, in the simple fact that while the employers had obtained munificence and become, as it were, millionaires, the workman had had to struggle on with only a bare subsistence, and had nothing to look forward to but to labour on to the end of his days, unless he should have had the forethought to ally himself to his trade society and obtain superannuation benefit, and thereby be, to a certain extent, independent of receiving parochial relief in his old age. This from the simple fact that, as a workman, he had not had a fair share of the profits of his labour. Not only had the employer had the advantage in a commercial point of view, but also in a political sense, for while the employer had had laws made to assist him in conducting his business, the workman had had laws made which would grind him lower than now if it were possible. (Applause.) Mr. Ward further said, "That unless a fairly just advantage be gained on both sides the one will leave the other to its own helplessness." It might have applied to the employer, but what chance had the workman had in the past of leaving the employer if he did not receive his fair share of the profits? He had had no chance of escaping from the iron heel of oppression, for what could he do single-handed against a combination of employers? But the time was fast approaching when not only would he be able to demand a fair day's wage for a fair day's work, but would also have the means to obtain it. (Hear, hear.) Mr. Ward said further, "That he need not say a word as to the powerlessness of capital without labour; but it is not so needless to ask what can labour do without capital?" thereby implying that labour was the dependent. But he forgot, or overlooked in the first part of his paper, that the workman was now to a great extent in a position to help himself, and not only to supply labour but to create capital. He alluded to co-operation, for as has been shown by late statistics in co-operation, the workmen were in a better position to compete with the capitalist than the capitalist to compete with them. What was to hinder trades' unions from using their extensive capital in co-operative works? The vast funds, increasing year by year, were they always to be wasted in fighting battles between employer and employed? No, for strikes in the past had been a loss on both sides, and what gain had been obtained had been of no account to balance with the expenditure; but it must be the study of the workmen in disputes in the future not only to stop the supply of labour to the employers, but to utilise that

E

labour and make it return as it were a hundred-fold instead of lying idle. (Applause.) Mr. Ward said, further, that there is a fundamental error into which many fall, which consists in supposing that capital and labour are the sum total of what is necessary to the production and distribution of wealth. Brainwork, anxiety, knowledge, inventive genius, administrative skill, and never-resting commercial activity, are elements which must not and cannot be ignored. He would try to deal with that, and also a remark which fell from Mr. Simons at the same time. Mr. Simons said that he could not agree with the title of Mr. Ward's paper, " Capital and Labour," but considered that it would have suited the case better had it been " Knowledge and Labour." He thought Mr. Simons must certainly be labouring under a very serious delusion, for he would imply by his words that labour was totally ignorant, and that it was only with the employer knowledge lay. He also quoted that " Knowledge is power." It was so, but it did not follow that the employer had all the knowledge — (hear, hear) — for of what power was labour without skill ? Or of what use was the labour to the employer if the employed did not combine knowledge with it ? (Hear, hear.) The employer could obtain mere labour from mechanical inventions, but of what use were those inventions without the knowledge of the mechanic to use them at the same time ? For what did the youth serve a term of apprenticeship but to obtain that knowledge or skill which, combined with his labour, would enable him in after years to obtain a livelihood ? (Hear, hear.) A workman's brainwork must not be ignored. Mr. Ward said also, " I must speak of trades' unions and federations of employers. So far as the object of trades' unions is to raise the working classes in the social scale and to resist oppression and injustice, my sympathy is with them, and I fully believe that their interests cannot be secured and protected single-handed. Combination is, therefore, justifiable and praiseworthy. No property could be more sacred than the faculties of a man's mind or the powers of his body, and he has a right in any way he may think proper to set his own price on his services, so long as he does not injure or interfere with the freedom of others." The point was in those last few words. He contended that they, as trades' unionsts, have the right to interfere with the action of others if they found the action of the few detrimental to the interests of

the majority of the trade at large—that they had the right to use
all lawful means of persuasion in their power.   Mr. Ward said, "I
may specially refer to the Criminal Law Amendment Act ;" so also
did Mr. Hancock.   He said he could not see that it was not equal
for all classes in its framing and wording, inasmuch as it did not
make special mention of trades' unions.   Now, if trades' unions were
things of the past, that accursed Act would never have been on the
statute-book of this country ; for it was specially directed against working class trades' unions, and they had direct proof that it was not allowed
to reach others than manual workers.   There were many cases which
could be quoted.   He contended that the working classes had just cause
to say that the Act was one-sided, and to demand its total repeal.   Mr.
Ward said, "I should like to ask whether the opposition of trades'
unions to piecework is wise ?"   He contended that the opposition to
piecework was wise, because those who had seen the working of it, as
he had, admitted that instead of improving any trade it degraded it, for
not only did it bring into the labour market inferior labour, but it also
had a tendency to lower wages.   For instance, when some employers had
agreed to a certain price, and found that the workman had earned more
than he would have done at day work in the same time, what did they
do but reduce the price ?   So they would do, until the iron heel of
oppression would make the workmen very slaves indeed.   Mr. Ward
believed that piecework and a system of contract were essential to secure
the interests of the general public.   He held that it was the very opposite
of being for the public good, for the public at large wished for a sound
principle, and not a rotten one, as undoubtedly piecework and contract
labour was.   (Applause.)   What did it interest the piece-worker or
contractor of what quality his work or material was, so long as it served
him until he got paid for it ?   He took no interest in his work being
sound, and his motto was for quantity, and not quality.   It was also to
the interests of the ratepayers that trades' unions should do their best to
prevent a few from reaping the benefits of the trade, by a course which
would bring semi-starvation to the remainder of the trade.   Did they
not, by persuading men to become members and partake of their benefits,
take some of the burden off the backs of the ratepayers, when the member was out of work, sick, or met with an accident, or death ?   So long

as he had health and strength so long would he oppose piecework, whether he occupied the position of employer or employed, for he was convinced that it was and had been a curse to those who had to live by their labour. (Applause.)

Mr. HUGH BROWNE said that as one rather placed between masters and men, he must say that both masters and men had had their cause well advocated. They were as much connected as the Siamese twins. There never yet was an employment not beneficial to employer and employed ; and they had to recognise the principle that both person and property should be at the absolute disposal of the man possessing one or the other, or both. Starting with the mutual benefit of employer and employed, what had hitherto been their relations ? It had been well contended by Mr. Albert Richards and others that they had seen legislation taking the side of the capitalist. Only about half a century ago Joseph Hume moved to inquire into the effect of combinations of labour —as to whether these combinations were in defiance of the law, and as to what were their results. The inquiry developed that in every large trade, where the men had united, their wages were from 5s. to 10s. a week higher than in the trades where the men had not united. (Hear, hear.) Upon this the speaker noticed the legislative action taken for the recognition of these combinations of labour. Having been recognised by the law, and these unions having achieved great power, they must not expect that power would be without misuse, and they had only to go back to the Sheffield inquiry a few years ago for instances. There it was shown that rattening was the common means for enforcing unionism, and it was vain to say that the power of unions had been without grievous misuse— that coercion was unknown. Mr. Chatwin had said that a man should be prevented interfering unduly with his own trade ; but was the weak man to be set over the strong, or were they to recognise that the strong always triumphed over the weak ? The skilled workman should always get the best wages. What was coercion ? For his own part, he recognised that every individual should do with his own person and property that which seemed to him good, so long as he did no wrong to those around him. (Hear, hear.)

THIRD NIGHT'S DISCUSSION.

(TUESDAY, APRIL 28, 1874.)

MR. HUGH BROWNE, in continuing the observations made by him at the previous meeting, commenced by saying that he had claimed to approach this subject somewhat as an outsider, and as one looking at it from a disinterested—or, at least, from a comparatively disinterested—point of view. The matter had been discussed very ably on the part of employers and workmen. He must recognise the manner in which our present has grown out of our past. In our own time, not very long ago, there was oppressive legislation with regard to combinations of labour ; but since the combination laws were abolished in 1824, the proper relations of masters and men had become more and more recognised—it had become more and more recognised that these classes were entitled to stand equal before the law. This, theoretically, had been done to a large extent. Practically, however, so far as laws must depend on prejudiced human nature, they never could have perfect equality. The utmost that could be done was for them to discuss trade matters, and they could do nothing better than let the masters and men meet together in this way, in order to lay before each other their mutual complaints ; and the good spirit shown throughout this discussion must be regarded with pleasure. (Hear, hear.) It must be admitted that there were several points as to which it was very difficult to form an outside opinion. One of the best possible evidences of the spirit shown was that no working men would attempt to justify the excesses and coercion which had been indulged in by unions. (Applause.) They might refer to those cases which had been only too frequent in Sheffield and in the brick trade, and other trades where there had been unions, some strong and some weak ; but, as it had been ably put by the men, such cases had been principally where unions were weak or non-existent. Where labour was organised into unions, he thought it a fair question to inquire whether there had not been less coercion, and whether excesses had not been rather where unions did not exist at all, or where they were exceedingly weak? (Hear, hear.) Acknowledging that there had been mistakes on both sides, they were examining the true relations of capital and labour. They had had certain theories put forward, or half put forward, with which he could not agree. For instance, they had had the illustration of the cakes, as to which surely if anything could with justice be advanced, it was that the bargain made to-day should be adhered to to-morrow. (Hear, hear.) Supposing an agreement was entered into by which the capitalist got many cakes, and the labourer only a few, he could not understand why the labourer should think it right to say, "We will have the cakes divided." (Hear, hear.) But they must also see whether or not the bargains themselves might be excessively restrictive, and here they came to the most difficult problems. Were capitalists justified in uniting to raise the rate of the market for their goods? He thought his hearers would agree that they were. Admit, then, that combinations among capitalists were perfectly legal and justifiable, even though the action taken by them should check trade and ruin competitors. Next they came to the question as to trades' unions—were so many unionists justified in saying, "We will not work with non-unionists?" This might seem rather a strong question to put, but, again, he asked, would they be justified in forcing these unionists to work with non-unionists? In his opinion, the natural answer to either question would be "No." It was hard for the non-unionist if, by the action of unionists, he was prevented from getting employment whereby to earn his bread, but in either of these cases how was it to be remedied? He was of opinion that it was difficult to apply a remedy by law. Law was one of those very flexible things which a judge, under the law of conspiracy for example, might stretch to mean almost anything. (Hear, hear.) They were, however, talking more for political economy. Law had its limits and was evil where it was futile, and he was afraid they must recognise the right of any body of men to say that they would not work with certain other men. He could see great injustice arising from it, yet the difficulties were so extreme, and he was afraid law was so ineffective in such cases, that they must leave it to the common sense of the community. There, and there only, he thought was the remedy. So far as he could understand, he did not see how they should compel unionists to work beside non-unionists. It had been said from time to time, " But there is this great contrast of wealth and poverty." There, again, they came to the matter of bargain, and the bargain made to-day, even where the capitalist got a great advantage, must be abided by to-morrow. Should they have laws to stimulate the aggregation of wealth, or its distribution ? He thought that the general action of laws should rather have a tendency to induce the distribution of wealth than its aggregation. (Applause.) Mr. Mather had ably spoken upon the landowners as a separate class of capitalists, but the subject was such an extensive one that he (the speaker) dare not enter upon it. He, therefore, omitted that question, with, however, a recognition of its vast importance, and they must treat the question of capital and labour as the question of the relations between masters and men in trade. He thought they must recognise the right of the unionist to regulate his labour as he pleased. They must not attempt to interfere by law in this matter, yet the unionist should see that political economy might dictate to him certain limits—not dictated to him by legal enactments. No doubt it was a pity to see one man possessed of an enormous amount of wealth, while, at the same time, there were thousands of others in want. The apparent hardship resulted from the artificial state of society. In trade the reward of energy was always to get the advantage, which was the high and necessary price we pay for energy and skill, and without that high price he thought we should fail to get either. Capital, also, was skilled labour when well applied, and they must see that all the great disparity of fortune was the result of the working out of the laws of common bargaining. He could not help complimenting both masters and men on the spirit which they had displayed, and laid stress on the importance of recognising absolute justice, absolute equality before the law. But taking all these matters, and admitting that there must be hardships, and that the picture drawn by Mr. Start of the abolition of poverty was too Utopian ; they would always have great wealth, and with it great poverty as a contrast. Yet it was not that the working men were poorer than formerly—it was that the capitalist was richer. (Hear, hear.) The working man generally got good food. There were very many opportunities which he had of culture, and even of luxury, which our forefathers were ignorant of. Therefore, they must not take it as a fact that labour was always getting poorer because the capitalists were getting richer. He thought it would be found, on comparison with what we call "the good old times," that labour was gaining a better position day by day—(hear, hear)—and it should have a fair representation before the law in Parliament and elsewhere, when such laws as the law of conspiracy and the denial of legal protection to union funds would be impossible, and when such decisions as that in the gas stokers' case should be abolished. (Applause.) Passing from Mr. Justice Brett, the speaker continued that it might be seen that in many things they could make various improvements. The great thing was to recognise the equality of all before the law—to attain as much justice as was possible between man and man, and then, in his opinion, energy would have its fair recompense and reward. Yet there would still be great wealth and great poverty. (Hear, hear.) It might be that still they would have such cases as that of the dying cotton spinner exclaiming, "I thank Thee, O God, that the hard struggle of living is at last over," and he was afraid that we cannot avoid hardships, some of a most distressing kind. The Malthusian doctrine had never been fairly overturned, and so long as we have a growing population we shall always have the lower strata of society more or less tending to poverty. It must be recognised that hardship was a matter from which we cannot escape, and that the hardships of life will be unequally distributed throughout society, but the fair effort of energy in every class ought to be rewarded. Let master and man have good and friendly feelings towards each other, and we shall then do something to rise as a nation—we shall do the utmost it is possible to do, and more than it would be Utopian to attempt. (Loud applause).

Mr. EDMUND HART said he had attended more for the purpose of listening than speaking. He would observe at the outset, while there might be differences of opinion on the subject of capital and labour, there could be none as to the paper read by Mr. Ward—that it displayed an amount of concentration of thought rarely equalled. (Hear, hear.) He would just allude to the observations made by Mr. Start, who was the first to rise from the opposition benches. His speech contained many complaints that labour was at the mercy of capital. He stated that capital had had all the consideration—all the protection of the Legislature, and the grasping haste of the capitalists to get rich deprived labour of its legitimate rights." Facts would prove that nine-tenths of the employers of labour connected with three of our most important trades, namely, the machinists, lace manufacturers, and builders, had risen from the ranks of labour—not by combinations or trade unions, but by their own independent action and perseverance. While labour had accomplished all this, he affirmed that labour was not in that deplorable condition some would have them believe. As to capital having all the legislative protection, he believed the legislation of the past thirty years had been of the most equitable and beneficent character. It had accomplished more for labour than any other class. By Act of Parliament free trade was established, conferring benefits to all classes. Taxes on knowledge repealed, trades' unions confirmed, working hours limited, reduction of taxation on articles of domestic food and diet, the enfranchisement of the working classes, giving them an equality of electoral power with their employers, all accomplished by Act of Parliament. Mr. Start might have said with truth that the employers are in some degree at the mercy of the employed, by not having the liberty to employ whom they choose. Mr. Hancock made some statements as to the Criminal Law Amendment Act. The drift of that gentleman's statement was that there was nothing partial in that enactment—that unionists, non-unionists, masters, and men of all grades were equally liable to pains and penalties. Mr. Start stated that many were born in this country who were never asked whether they would be born, a condition of birth incident to all countries ; and he did not suppose they would get an intelligent answer if they asked such a question. (Laughter.) I think Mr. Start would not ignore parental responsibility, except to desire that the condition of the uncared-for portion of our population should have the consideration of trade unionists. Whether it was right to debar them from the means of obtaining a future maintenance by enforcing restrictions upon their opportunities of learning a craft whereby to obtain their daily bread. Mr. Albert Richards commenced by praising Mr. Ward's paper, but added that it contained just grounds of unfairness. He (the speaker) considered that unfairness did not form one particle of the paper. Mr. Richards stated that they had piles of wealth and millions of paupers. Wealth or capital, by its employment, was the primary antidote to pauperism. 'Twas not by trade unions, or agencies of that class, that the evils of pauperism would be materially decreased. Intemperance and idleness were the chief causes of pauperism.

> " He who lacks, for dread of daily work,
>   And his appointed task would shirk,
>   Commits a folly and a crime ;
>   A soulless slave, a paltry knave,
>   A clog upon the wheel of time.
>   With work to do, and health in store,
>   The man's unworthy to be free
>   Who will not give, that he may live,
>   His daily work for daily fee."

Paupers did not consist of men who desired to work. (Hear, hear.) The vast proportion of sober and industrious workmen need not dread the fear of the workhouse, if they would exercise their powers with perseverance and steady aim. Even if they did not succeed to a distinguished mark, they would obtain respect and honour—(applause)—and remember this :—

> " We must all be up and stirring,
>   With determination true ;
>   Young men, old men,
>   Rich men, poor men,
>   All have got their work to do."

There was no royal road to affluence.

> " In life's earnest battle they only prevail,
>   Who daily march onward, and never say fail."

The only way was that marked out by the Almighty, by following which men might hope to benefit themselves. Its guide-posts were self-improvement, industry, perseverance, and economy. (Loud applause).

Mr. RICHARD LAMB (Amalgamated Society of Operative Tailors) stated that he had listened attentively to the last speaker, whom he had known from boyhood. He knew that gentleman had been struggling hard for many years, but, he also knew, had not realised anything like

the amount of capital realised by some others who had not worked half
so hard. Reference had been made to the number of employers in the
various branches of trade who had sprung from the ranks of labour, but,
for his own part, he would say that he considered it was not possible for
all men to be employed. He should like Mr. Hart to remember that he
had scarcely ever known a journeyman to get rich, and a man had to be
an employer before he got on in the world. Gigantic fortunes, princely
residences, and vast landed estates obtained in an ordinary life-time,
must of necessity be the result of exorbitant profits. And yet the
possessors of these easily-acquired fortunes could be counted by their
thousands, and the bulk of them started life with little or nothing. The
works of art alone that adorned their dwellings, would cost more than
any working man could realise in a life-time. There were, no doubt, a
variety of ways in which this could be done. For example, a man
might possibly do it by cringing to those placed above him, though for
his own part he should not like to secure personal advancement at the
sacrifice of self-respect. (Hear, hear.) He found, from a pamphlet he
held in his hand, that the writer said contentions between employer and
employed were not by any means of modern date. The earliest record,
it appeared, that we have, was so far back as 3,500 years ago.
(Laughter.) It was stated to be when Jacob quarrelled with Laban
over the question of wages. (Renewed laughter.) So it would be seen
from this, that the world had been continually progressing in the matter
of these disputes. It was, no doubt, going back a long way with respect
to this constant strife between employer and employed. He thought,
however, that surely it was high time there was a new era. (Hear,
hear.) With Mr. Ward, and with other gentlemen who had spoken in
the course of the discussion, he thought it was most desirable that both
classes should meet upon one common platform in order to discuss dis-
passionately the merits of this important question. For any one to maintain that capital should have such a great share in the profits resulting
from labour, he considered to be a great mistake. Dr. Angus Smith,
F.R.S., in a lecture delivered before the members of the Manchester
Philosophical Society, said, "Supply and demand were terms used to
skim over great difficulties. They have been treated as merely physical,
but when moral considerations enter, supply and demand alter their con-

ditions, and *the physical laws must give way*, because there are moral feelings in men stronger than their love of gain." Then Sir Archibald Alison said :—" I think trades' unions are not only proper, but a necessary balance of the fabric of society. Without them, capital would become far too powerful, and the workmen would be much beaten down. The men have reason to believe that if they were deprived of the power of combination, their wages would be gradually brought down to such a point that they would be reduced to the former condition of the serfs in Russia." Mr. J. Ruskin, in a paper on " Wealth and its Distribution," said :—" The idea that direction can be given for the gaining of wealth, irrespective of the consideration of its moral sources, or that any general or technical law of purchase or gain can be set down for national practice, is, perhaps, the most insolently futile of all that ever beguiled men through their vices. So far as I know, there is not in history the record of anything so disgraceful to the human intellect as the modern idea that the commercial text, *buy in the cheapest market and sell in the dearest*, represents an available principle of national economy. This supply and demand argument is especially the mercantile form of theft, consisting of taking advantage of a man's necessities, in order to obtain his labour at a reduced price." He could prove that it was done in this country to a considerable extent—for instance, taking machinery to another country where labour is badly paid, as Saxony, Belgium, and other places. The work there made was frequently of inferior quality, and was often sold as goods properly made in England and America, where skilled artisans were employed and properly remunerated for their labour. That was unmanly in two ways. First, they complained when a scarcity of labour took place—they grumbled at the heavy rates ; whereas, if it could be ascertained, it was by the withdrawal of labour to the sources above referred to ; and, secondly, to call them paupers when they had no possible chance of avoiding it. Should it not be attributed to their want of feeling in the matter ? Supposing, for instance, that an employer realised about 50 per cent. profit. If he took the whole of that, and at the same time gave a man whom he employed poor wages, though it might be rather strong language to use, he affirmed that the man so employed was deliberately robbed. There could be no mistake about it in his mind. But if the employer gave to his employed what was fair the case of course was altogether different—if, say, at the end of the year they were given something out of the profits actually realised, he did not say that the employer should not take the greatest share for himself. Now, some observations had been made with reference to the subject of the hours of labour—with reference to long hours of labour. He should on this point quote from Mr. Brassey, who as his hearers all knew, was an eminent man, and one who had made a great fortune. Had this been done by employing cheap labour? Decidedly not. Or was it done by getting his employed to work excessive hours? Decidedly not. He found that he had always been best helped, or best served, and had positively realised the most money, when he had employed good labour at moderate hours. (Hear, hear.) He believed himself, with Mr. Brassey, that the best labour would always get the best price, and that this was a necessary condition. Supposing a man was worth for his labour 10s. a-day, then he should have it without any restriction being imposed upon him. (Hear, hear.) There was another point as to which he desired to say one or two words. They might blame trades' unions for acts of coercion, which he regretted as much as any one, but, on the other hand, they should in common fairness look at what had in many cases been the conduct of the masters. He referred to such conduct as writing about a man to another employer, or to their employers, "Do not employ so-and-so—he is an agitator." He would ask, was not this worthy of the name of conspiracy? (Hear, hear.) For himself, he was inclined to think so. In this way the man would probably be compelled to become a pauper, or at least the consequences to him were very serious. He did not think that a reasonable number of apprentices in any trade was to be objected to, and he did not think that any trade unionist would not consent to it. But surely the question was one of importance. What, he asked, could be thought of swamping a place with apprentices? For a man to be thrown out of employment in this way he considered, after that man had served a term of years to learn his trade, monstrous. He hoped that the matter would be borne in mind, and taken into consideration by his hearers, for it must be admitted that it was well deserving of thoughtful attention. It was a good thing that they should meet together in a friendly manner to discuss their grievances. Take the case of the agricultural labourers. He did not think that there was any one present who had not the warmest sympathy with them. (Hear, hear.) As so much had been said in reference to trades' unions, let them speak of some of the good qualities of those organisations. When they obtained money they were not close-fisted with it, and he should like those who had much of it to bear that fact in mind, and follow their example. (A laugh.) He would say to every working man, if he had a society belonging to his trade, let him join it. To do so was eminently to his advantage. He referred to a pamphlet written by Mr. W. H. Wood, Secretary to the Manchester and Salford Trades' Council, which, he said was well worth perusing. Mr. Ward, in the paper which he had read, quoted from Mr. Ruskin. But Mr. Thomas Hill said that in no case had he known of such an advance in wages as had been obtained by domestic servants, and that this class of persons had no union. He wished to be allowed to say, however, that they had a union at Leamington about the same time as the Agricultural Labourers' Union was formed. (Hear, hear.) It was seen, he imagined, that that union would be a very strong one, and accordingly the employers of the servants raised their wages voluntarily, which he considered very thoughtful of them. (Laughter.) He was of opinion that the action was wise. (Cheers).

Mr. CHARLES MORETON said that as a representative of the stonemasons, there were a few motives which had actuated him in accepting the position he then occupied. The first was to comply with the invitation kindly forwarded by that club, the second was in order to advocate the cause of the class to which he belonged, and the third was that he thought he might obtain much valuable information. He was reminded, as to the consideration of this subject, of the artists who, going to sketch a particular landscape, did so, each from a different stand-point. (Hear, hear.) So it had been, he thought, with the various speakers, and he might say that each had presented a different view to their minds. In Mr. Ward's paper he read, " It is stated by the theoretical political economist that each is entitled to what he can obtain, and that the laws regulating supply and demand will, in the long run, redress all injustice." Now, to his mind, these laws had been a long time in redressing, for instance, the injustice of the agricultural labourer. It seemed to him that they wanted a more speedy remedy. (Hear, hear.) It must be seen there were many advantages in connection with trades' unions. Mr. Ward said, "I must now emphatically condemn many of the acts which have been, in the past, more or less associated with trades' unions." But in their general laws they did not sanction any violence, and, therefore he thought it was wrong for the author of the paper to condemn the trades' unionists unless he knew that their general laws advocated, or at least countenanced, anything of the kind. (Hear, hear.) Supposing, by way of illustration, that any gentleman belonging to that club committed himself, the town would not, on that account, condemn the club, but only the gentleman who had committed the act. Precisely the same argument held good with reference to trades' unions. If any individual member committed himself, they must not, therefore, condemn unions as a body. Accordingly, he thought that any such position fell to the ground. Next, "I fully believe that the interests of working men cannot be secured and protected single-handed. Combination is therefore justifiable, and even praiseworthy." There was another quotation which he would here make : "If a hundred men may combine, as I contend they may, to set a price on their own labour, it by no means follows that they should be allowed to dictate to fifty others, or to one other, the price which they demand." In looking at this question, he could not but remember that, as he thought, only one-third of the adult population of this country were entitled to vote, and had the power to make laws, or return representatives for that purpose, over all the rest. He believed, however, that two-thirds of any trade might make rules to regulate that trade, and to fix the amount of wages to be received. There were individuals who had not sufficient moral courage to stand up and ask for just remuneration for their labour. There were others who, under certain circumstances, would accept a lower price than they were worth, perhaps thinking that by taking a situation under price they would secure longer work. There had been numerous instances in his own trade. He was of opinion that trades' unions had a right to regulate the wages any of their members should receive, and Mr. Ward himself acknowledged that, single-handed, they could not get justice done to them. Next, speaking of the appointment of a Royal Commission as to the laws affecting labour, Mr. Ward went on to say, "I have no doubt that in consequence much light will be thrown on the true state of the case, and particularly on such acts as picketing, watching, and besetting men who accept situations which have been left by trades' unionists on strike." As to picketing and watching and besetting men, he did not think that if any body of men marched through this town without a breach of the peace, the police would think of apprehending them. Yet it seemed that if there was a contention between employers and employed, supposing a man walked about the street he might be apprehended as watching and besetting certain other individuals. For trades' unions pickets did very much as sentinels for an army during a campaign. It was admitted that but for organisation they would not be in the position which they occupied at the present day. Trades' unions had been brought about, not without a struggle, or without sacrifice, on the part of the members. Some had suffered imprisonment, some had endured privation to this end, and for one man to supplant another, that man supplanted thought in seeking to prevent it he was doing what was just and right. This individual, a non-unionist, was actually selling his birthright, as it were, for a mess of pottage, and positively doing an injury to the rising generation by selling his labour at a less price than was fair and proper. He maintained that the non-unionist owed a debt of gratitude to the unionist. Mr. W. A. Richards had said that the losses under the head of strikes counter-balanced the good results accomplished by their instrumentality. Possibly, but the same argument might be applied to all movements for ameliorating their social condition, or to many of them. He considered that in the past trades' unions had been as much a necessity as war had been a necessity with the different nations. (Hear, hear.) Then Mr. Ward, speaking as to piecework, said, "I should like to ask whether the opposition of the unions to piecework is wise. Should not greater diligence afford a claim to higher wages?" The experience of stonemasons had been that piecework brought about a system of sub-contracting, which caused the thing to be riddled and riddled until, when the journeyman was reached, it had to go through a very fine sieve. (A laugh.) Some, too, would work excessively hard, and to an extent not physically to their advantage. These were some of the reasons why piecework was being endeavoured to be abolished in his trade, and he thought wisely, seeing that individuals would work unnecessarily long hours, thus keeping others out of employment. There was another quotation :—" I think such action as practically leads to the paying of all hands alike, or which sets a limit to the amount of work a man shall perform, is opposed to the general interest." To some extent he quite endorsed this sentiment, but the employers who had generally complained of having so many inferior men seemed to speak as if the majority of the men were inferior. It should be borne in mind, too, that there were employers who had not sufficient conscientiousness, and who would wish an individual to work for less wages than he was worth. Then as to over-work, he had seen men who could scarcely walk off the ground upon which they had been engaged. He held that it was better for twenty men to be under-worked than one over-worked, and regard should be had for the economy of human nature. He thought the spirit of the agricultural labourers and others, who were emigrating and leaving home and country to find employment in another land, did not much indicate a spirit of idleness. Surely it was rather the reverse. He would admit that there were idle workmen, but there were also idle gentlemen. (Laughter.) Again, " Another aspect of this same point must now be considered, viz., the opinion held by many that the reduction of the hours of labour must of necessity improve the condition of workmen." If, supposing in the case of America, they worked fourteen hours a day, it was no reason why the same should be done here. Rather let such a condition of things in America be remedied. It was desirable that no class should be over-worked. As to the reduction of the hours of labour, several points were to be looked at. Take, as an illustration, men running a race, and it was found that a short race was run much faster than a long one. With reference to arbitration, he would like to say here that he should wish a system of arbitration to be brought about, as the sooner differences were settled by intellect rather than by any other means, the better. (Applause.) He believed in a system of arbitration, but there was the fact that many employers were opposed to it, and he had met them ; and besides, there were working men also opposed to it. Even though, under such a system, they did not get all that was asked for, it would be better than to have continual striking. He would like to go in a peace-

F.

able way, and he agreed with Mr. Ward on this subject. He liked the
language of that gentleman as to co-operation. Much, he believed
would be done in this direction owing to trades' unions, and he thought
that it was the only means of bringing about anything like an equality
of labour and wealth. It was, he believed, largely in the power of the
working classes to raise themselves. (Hear, hear.) They had, in his
opinion, every facility for introducing a system of co-operation, and in
time he was inclined to think that they would all become amalgamated
in it, when the best men would be in the best position. It was to be
hoped that working men would turn their attention more to this principle of co-operation. He agreed with Mr. Ward generally on the
subject of taxation, and approved of a judicious system of indirect taxation on articles which might be regarded more as luxuries than necessaries. And then this matter wanted looking at in a moral point of
view, and to him it was a most important question. A man's life was
not simply made up of pounds, shillings, and pence. He had something
more to live for. Mr. Ward said, and well said, " 'For one man to seek
his own good at the expense of his neighbour's welfare has been, since
dust was first made flesh, the curse of man ; and to do as you would be
done by, the one source of all natural blessing.' This is the Communism
of the Father of us all, and his executive power is all-sufficient to enforce
his law." This he could endorse. Where nations had acted contrary to
moral laws they had had to pay the penalty. That applied to employer
as well as employed. As to the difference in the wages of working men,
each wanted sufficient food and a proper house to live in without in-
fringing the laws of health, to have which each individual must be
remunerated accordingly. He should like unionists to endeavour to set
an example to the employers, and let them meet and discuss the point,
and see whether they could not do something to raise those who were
lower down in the scale as to payment. He believed it was impossible
to expect equality with regard to men's abilities, but he believed that
something might be done so far as concerned the distribution of wealth.
He felt deeply indebted to the club for having the privilege of attending
to speak on this important question. If he had at all failed, he trusted
that his hearers would accept the will for the deed. He hoped that there
would be more of these meetings, and whether he himself attended or not,

doubtless others better calculated to defend the cause of trades' unions, or deal with the relations of capital and labour, would be present, but he had done his best. (Loud applause).

Mr. THOMAS SMITH said there were a variety of matters upon which he thought stress should be laid, deserving consideration as to this question of the relations of capital and labour. Capital was the basis on which material civilization rested, and without accumulated wealth there could be no material civilization. It seemed to him that the first requisite to the accumulation of wealth was that man should be possessed of foresight, and of sufficient self-denial to act upon that, and practice it. (Hear, hear.) When men lived on the animals they caught, which were wild, a man might catch a wild animal with young, and he might say to himself, having regard for the future, " I had better let the young ones grow up rather than kill them." But all would not do so—all would not be possessed of the same foresight, or some might not have the self-denial to practice it. The working classes, he observed in passing, had to suffer much more than any class, but theirs was enforced denial, and not self-denial. The result of what he had given as an illustration would be that in time of scarcity, when some who had not accumulated any flocks or herds were pressed for food, the man who had accumulated food in such a way would obtain for himself, as a consideration for parting with some of that which he had accumulated, the labour of others. From all this they could see how the relations between capital and labour would gradually grow up. The same thing held good all through this contest, and from that time until now had been irrepressible. The man employed thought that he did not get sufficient for what work he did, but the employer thought quite otherwise, and so long as there were those who had wealth and those who had not, this would continue. (Hear, hear.) In the present state of society men might start poor, accumulate wealth, and become employers ; and the fact of their doing so would suffice to show that they were possessed of forethought and self-denial. On the other hand, they saw men who for lack of these qualities lost the advantages of which they were possessed by birth, and sank down in society. In the present state of society that was inevitable. It certainly did not seem to him that all could equally be

endowed with these qualities, though more persons might be so endowed
than now, as the result of education ; but if we were to wait until all
had these qualities we should have to wait a very long time. (Hear,
hear.)   But so long as the existing condition of society lasted, this contention between the two classes must continue.   The question arose,
How were they to obviate it ?   Co-operation, in his opinion, would do
much, and even trades' unions, and the cultivation of habits of forethought and saving ; but there would still be a large class remaining.
In this country he believed that working men had fewer habits of saving
than was the case with their class in almost any other country.   They
had certainly less than in America—he believed, also, less than in all
the continental countries, and he thought it largely originated from the
fact that in those countries land was within the reach of the labourers.
The land system here made it almost impossible for the labourer to
emancipate himself while he stayed in the country.   But on the
continent a man working and saving a little money had opportunities of
buying plots of land of various sizes, in accordance with his means.
Besides, transfer was exceedingly cheap and easy.   They must bear in
mind that before the system of serfdom was abolished—which dated, on
the continent, from the time of the French Revolution of 1789—the
people had not these opportunities, and the labourers could not make
themselves capitalists and their own employers.   If, here, they could
give the labourers the same opportunities of becoming their own employers, it would no doubt be productive of the same results as elsewhere ; for he thought it was pretty generally acknowledged that working men in this country were the least saving of any in the world.
Some of the speakers who had preceded him disavowed that they were
Communists.   Now he himself was a Communist, and he was an
advocate both of the Commune of Paris and also of Communism, which
were two different things.   In reference to the subject of co-operation,
it was one method for enabling men to become capitalists associatively.
Supposing a thousand men were living in common, and the bulk of them
had the qualities of forethought and self-denial of which he had spoken
sufficiently to accumulate property, they would be able to influence the
rest if acting associatively, and able to prevent them squandering their
wealth for want of forethought.   Acting in a mass, it would not be abso-

lutely necessary for every individual to be endowed with these qualities. Though it might confer upon them a benefit which did not spring directly from their own efforts, to do so would only be doing unto others what they would have others do unto themselves. (Hear, hear.) It was well known that inventors—and they were a very useful class—had added enormously to the wealth of all countries, but frequently they had very little saving about them, and nearly all died poor. What they had done was very beneficial, yet they had not this quality of self-denial, or that other quality of forethought, which would lead them to take full advantage of their inventions. Although these men added as much wealth to the country as any amount of energy and business talent, still they derived no advantage commensurate with the benefits they conferred. Under the system of Communism, however, they would do so. Take, say, a town like Nottingham. It did already own considerable property in the shape of houses and land, and contemplated the purchase of the local gas and water works, in addition to which it would shortly have various sets of schools belonging to it. That was Communism—the owning of property by the community instead of by private individuals. There were, of course, many in Nottingham who did not practice self-denial, but they would have the benefit of these works nevertheless. Society could not be carried on except by labour, and it was only fair that every man should do a portion of it. Labour had an elevating effect upon the human family. As matters stood at present, one class had to do the work, and did not feel the beneficial effects of having much interest in property. The capitalist—or at least he who lived upon the interest on investments—must be aware that he was consuming wealth without rendering help to produce any. (Hear, hear.) If labour was this very honourable thing, surely it would be well that an individual like that should have some of the honour. (Laughter.) The possession of capital had also a beneficial effect, morally and intellectually, upon character. Why not confer on all the advantages of both labour and capital, and let every one have his share of the good things? Under this system of Communism—which, it should be understood, might take a thousand developments—it was certain that the amount of labour requiring to be performed by each person would not hurt any one. (Laughter and applause).

FOURTH NIGHT'S DISCUSSION.

(TUESDAY, MAY 5, 1874.)

Mr. THOMAS SMITH, continuing his remarks from last week, said the question before his mind was, in what manner to reconcile the interests of both capital and labour. Many men were yet what he should call uncivilized, for they had not the qualities upon which civilization was based—the qualities of prudence and foresight. Just as, in an unsettled and uncivilized state of society, a man lived upon the animal he caught until he could catch another, so very large numbers of persons, after working all week for wages, when they caught their buffalo on Saturday night, spent it before they could catch another. (Laughter.) Now, if it had not been for the savers, the old state of society would have gone on ; and many men, at least among the agricultural population, have more to endure, and less pleasures, than the men who lived in this condition of nature. They had to work harder, and often fared harder ; and though men in such a state of society had frequently to suffer great privations, the same held good with regard to working men in case of slackness of trade, sickness, or at other times. The saving classes, who had so altered the condition of society as to impose these worse conditions upon the non-savers, had certain duties devolving upon them. If the whole of the country were still wild, of course the population would be smaller. As to resistance to new and improved machinery, where the working classes had done this on account of the displacement of labour, they had not been more stupid or determined in that resistance than the upper classes had been with respect to political and social reforms which would be beneficial to the working classes. So this kind of thing had more or less pervaded both classes. Almost all the improvements in our political and social position had been bitterly resisted by the upper classes. This brought him to the fact that the principle upon which society was based is wrong, because we have individuality of interest—not mutuality of interest. (Hear, hear.) Instead of our interests being the same they are antagonistic, and it must be so while society is based upon the principle of competition instead of mutuality. The impossibility of making peace between the two classes had, he thought, been shown by the long antagonism which had existed, and the failure of the many efforts made with the view of producing good relations. A man might at one time think that what he received was a fair rate of wages ; but circumstances alter—trade becomes more brisk, or something else occurs, and he demands higher wages. That led to a fresh quarrel, often to a strike, and, eventually, there was another compromise ; yet it was only a compromise, for if circumstances should change, either master or man would insist upon an alteration to suit that change which had been brought about. It was the result of the fact that their interests were divergent, and they would always quarrel as they thought they could insist upon a fresh compromise. A friend of his once told a tale about a joiner, and it appeared that there had been a quarrel between the joiners and their masters, the former wanting 25s. a week. Now this particular joiner referred to, in speaking of the matter, declared that this amount of 25s. was fair before God and man. Ultimately, the men got it, as the result of a strike that took place. Some time afterwards his friend met the joiner again, who said that he was going to America because there he could get something like 36s. a week for his labour. Upon this, his (the speaker's) friend said, "Why, I thought you told me that 25s. was fair before God and man. Are you going to rob some one in America ?" (Laughter.) If a man saw that there was an advantage to be got, he would get it if he could, and the same with the master ; and it would always be so while the interests of the two were different, because people would naturally think of their own interests first. As to the question of saving, so far as concerned any country the town populations had less inducements to save than the country populations, and where land could be easily obtained and the transfer laws were such that small quantities of land might be made over without the process being a burden. (Hear, hear.) If they looked at the artisan population of other countries, as a rule they were less saving than the country population ; but in this country it was impossible for the agricultural labourer to save anything. Take, however, the position of France or of Germany, where land could easily be obtained if a man had saved a few pounds. In this way a man with a small sum of money could buy a plot of land, and he had the opportunity of employing his own labour for himself. The greatest inducement for people to save was that they might employ their own labour for themselves. They might utilise much labour, and the inducements under these circumstances were far greater to save in the country than in the town. Supposing a working man in Nottingham had £10 or £20, what could he put it in—how could he very profitably invest it ? He could not by its means utilise his own labour for himself. He could not use this small amount of capital so as to have the benefit of his own exertions, and he therefore repeated that the inducement to save was less with town than with country populations. But as he had said, in England the agricultural population had neither inducement nor opportunity to save. He might refer to unions as an exemplification of this principle of saving, and here foresight was exercised with the view of providing for contingencies. Besides, there was the principle of self-denial, which was practised by the members who paid into the unions. Many argued that unions would not raise wages, that the law of supply and demand would put wages up or down in spite of unions. It had, no doubt, its influence, both on men who acted associatively and individually. Talking about unions, the members having capital were armed with both labour and capital to fight against capital alone. Thus they must have an advantage which they could not have if they only had their labour with which to fight against capital, in which case, unless the demands of the capitalists were very urgent, they would be quickly forced into submission. In the present state of society, the only qualities which appeared worthy of rewarding well were the money-getting qualities. A man, in order to get money, must have foresight, and what were generally termed business qualities. There were, however, many other qualities beneficial to society. He had previously referred to the class of inventors, scientific men, and writers generally, including poets and all intellectual workers, who usually get paid very badly indeed for their labour. Still, they were just as beneficial to society, and often more so, than was mere business talent. He held that under the present condition of society, men did not get rewarded in comparison with the benefits they conferred. The man with business qualities got reward heaped upon him, very frequently, until he was almost buried alive. (Laughter.) But not so with those who had not those qualities. And yet, as to the amount of toil they had in managing their business, every one knew that nineteen-twentieths of business was just as much routine as the work of the labourer. (Hear, hear.) Where there was great anxiety and thought, it was usually in speculative enterprises. In a fancy trade, like that of one of the staples of the town of Nottingham, there would be more anxiety, and trouble, and risk of loss ; but the profits were larger in proportion than in some trades, which, he should think, were almost all routine, and which could not require very great abilities. But under the system he advocated, that of Communism, where property would be held by society as a whole, and not by the individual, these abilities of the business man would still be required, and such men would doubtless get very much the same positions, though not, perhaps, quite so much pay. (Laughter.) Yet the pay would not be quite so bad as that which inventors frequently received, and they would not die in a workhouse, but would be sure of a comfortable living. In addition, they would have less anxiety, and that would be a great compensation for people who thought that under such a state of things as Communism they would not get a fair reward for their labour. Men would have much less anxiety, not only for themselves, but also for their families. As an illustration, a man might accumulate wealth, but yet not be at all sure that his children would be able to keep it ; and there was often a good deal of anxiety as to what would be the result, in children, of the want of provident qualities. But under a system of Communism, so long as they performed their fair share of work, they would be certain of a proper existence. It was true that a man might feel his dignity or pride lowered if he had to be equal with the rest of his fellow-men, though that would not be a loss to him, for vices, it seemed to him, were only virtues run to excesses. Gluttony was eating run to excess, and with regard to pride, it was but self-respect run mad. (Laughter.) He believed that every quality which man possessed, if properly used, was good in itself, and what was called vice was wholly the result of undue preponderance—of one getting the mastery. Then a

man might be a good business manager for other people, and have good
business qualities, though he could not manage for himself. He might
have order, and system, and all that kind of thing, but still perhaps be
deficient in foresight. He might not have sufficient self-control to
prevent him from spending money faster than he got it. Under Communism all the various qualities would be utilised. Men would find
their place, and would be able to devote those qualities to the good of
the community, instead of the money-making quality being regarded as
the one virtue of society to be exalted as the great desideratum. As to
example, the case he was going to refer to was that of Christ and his
Apostles, who were Communists. No doubt his hearers were Christians,
or professed to be, whether they practised it or not—(laughter)—but all
might not know that Christ and his Apostles lived in common, so far as
their history was given in the New Testament; and they had not individual property. The early Christians, also, following their example,
lived in common, as might be seen from the example of Ananias and
Sapphira, who met with a measure of repression equal to any in modern
times against new ideas, for not fully adhering to the principles of
mutuality. The principle of Communism was taught and believed in by
the early Christians, from the fact that they practised it, and for ages by
the monks. It was a common argument against Communism that it
would lead to universal beggary and ruin, and he did not know what.
Yet there could be cited thousands of instances were Communism had
answered in a material point of view. It might be supposed that the
monks comprised men of different qualities, some thoughtful and careful,
and some reckless; but through the whole course of Christianity they
found that these men who lived associatively continually became richer.
If a number of men were taken and placed together under this principle,
such as were for accumulating and saving would be more powerful
in the society than those who were less provident. The monks, so far
as concerned their different qualities, would be just as various as society
at the present day; but so far as material wealth was concerned, they
were always successful. He supposed that none were opposed more to
what was called Communism than the aristocracy of this country; but
the very basis upon which the aristocracy rested was Communism more
or less. By the law of primogeniture and entail they endeavoured to

keep their estates to the eldest son, and practised Communism so far as it would protect and benefit themselves. The object of Communism was to confer on all men the advantages of civilization—the advantages of accumulated wealth. Not only so, but to insure to all, through life, that they shall not come to poverty as long as they do their fair share of labour, and in old age. The aristocracy, by this law of primogeniture and entail, took the advantages themselves and threw the responsibility upon the community. When, however, it was attempted to apply the principle to the whole of society, they were denounced as enemies of society, and other things. From this it would be seen that people were willing to adopt these principles so far as they would suit themselves. With reference to the question of population, he thought that on the part of the founders of monastic orders it was a bold attempt to meet the population question; but from the laws of population not being then understood, and they being based upon celibacy, which was an unnatural state, they failed to solve that question; and he would remark that in all ages, Communists, both practical and theoretical—and they almost, if not they alone, till the present age—had tried more or less to deal with the population question. While, however, they had this system of competition, these evils would harrass society. Though some classes might think that they could protect themselves from the evils, if one class of society suffered, it more or less affected the whole. Take the case of the slaves in America. Before the civil war, one in eight were slaves, and formed a helpless, ignorant class. The civil war was the result of that slavery, and during that struggle as many able-bodied white men went to their graves as would be found in the four millions of slaves. For every able-bodied black man held in slavery, then, one able-bodied white man was killed, however much it was thought that they would escape from the penalty of inflicting slavery because of the weakness of their victims. As, when one part of the body was diseased, the whole of the body felt it and suffered, so, when one portion of society suffered under an evil of any kind, it would affect the whole of society, and he saw no way of avoiding it. A system of Communism was requisite to the end that society as a whole might be rescued from the evils existent, all deriving the advantages of the prudence and foresight exercised by the majority. Those classes who might not have the advantage of foresight and prudence could still by their labour produce wealth, and it was the distribution which was now the question of most importance. (Hear, hear.) Wealth enough could be produced, but its distribution was so bad. As they saw that the monks, who practised this principle of common property, grew rapidly in wealth, so no doubt it would be with society, notwithstanding that some were afraid to do so would lead to universal ruin. So far as the principle was concerned, rich men would not be compelled to enter into Communism. The application of that principle to individuals would be voluntary. Social reforms could not be gained by violence, though he believed that political reforms were always got by force, or the fear of it. The question of the rights of conscience, or that of serfdom or slavery, for instance, might and could be met by force, and in such cases this was generally the case ; but social reforms could not be conquered by force, they must spring from intelligence. (Hear, hear.) If men in favour of Communism had the mastery of the country, they could not introduce that principle by simply having the Government in their own hands, as to do so the people must be prepared in their minds, and they could not force it upon them. Supposing the people said, " We don't want education," they could not be compelled to learn. A horse might be taken to water, but could not be made to drink. It was thought by many that Communists, of whom he was one, wished to force their principles upon society. Now he for one advocated force in regard to political reforms, when they could not be obtained without, but, as he had said, it was perfectly impossible for social reforms to be brought about by such means. If the rich thought they would not get their full rights, they need not go under this system of Communism. Yet if those who produced wealth liked to combine, as did the monks, they should do so, but not to compel any one to join them who did not choose. He was reminded as to the present state of society, of the anecdote of the Yankee lads who, after an hour's ex-changing of knives amongst themselves, found that each had profited by the transaction, getting back his own knife and fifty dollars. (Laughter.) By speculation persons simply " swapped " backwards and forwards, not in many cases making wealth even by the legitimate competitive system of producing wealth and making a profit. It simply meant the transfer of that which was produced from one man's pocket to another's, and no one was benefited except he who had the best of the bargain. A man would get the advantage with superior sharpness, and, when he accumulated a fortune, it was looked upon as a wonderful thing ; but it was of no benefit to society, although, under the present state of society, rewarded very highly. As to the great mass of society, they were concerned in having as much wealth produced as possible, and in having the wealth produced distributed as equally as possible. (Hear, hear.) In reference to rewarding people for their peculiar abilities, it was said that all would be so equal that a man with peculiar abilities would not be rewarded properly. He thought there should be a distinction as to what rewarding was. If a man exerted himself physically to produce wealth, the natural reward was that he had the wealth for his sustenance and comfort. But if a man did mental labour, whether in shape of organisation, or in thinking, or in scientific discovery, the proper reward was what he should call mental reward—that was, the respect and honour with which he was looked upon by the rest of his fellows, and the consciousness of doing good work, and adding to the knowledge of the race. They knew that the bulk of such persons did not get very much now, and he thought that Milton got only £5 for writing his "Paradise Lost ;" so these persons would not be much worse off. (Laughter.) Of course, one class would, apparently, suffer—the men with this ability to make bargains. The compensation to them would be the release from anxiety, both with regard to themselves and their children. He would put it generally that physical work should be paid for by physical rewards, and mental work by mental rewards. One more observation, and he had done. They heard much about "public opinion," and, doubtless, there was much public opinion which was not private opinion. Men often had opinions privately which they did not express publicly. Many, privately, were in favour of the principle of Communism who did not say so publicly, and it would be a great deal better if public opinion and private opinion were more allied. People held opinions in favour of reform, but did not express them, though to do so would be better. It would be far better for them to come forth publicly and state their opinions at first, when, if they deserve to be exploded, let them be exploded, or adopted if worthy of adoption. He held that, under this system of which he was speaking, all kinds of merit would be properly rewarded—would get the reward proper for the kind of exertion used. While this system was not adopted—so long as this principle of antagonism continued—so long as every man's hand was against every other man, and all were striving against each other, they would inevitably have this system of eternal war. (Hear, hear.) They might as well attempt to mix oil and water as to try and combine the interests of employer and employed. Before the results desired could be attained, they must alter the principle upon which society was based. The fruit produced would be according to the tree, and before peace could be obtained society must be based upon a principle under which the interests of all would be similar. Peace would then follow naturally —the condition of things would be vastly improved, and not simply differences bridged over. It would then be as natural to practice living in peace, as to look after one's-self. Under the present system of society, the commandment "Love ye one another," should rather be, "Do ye one another." (Laughter.) In conclusion, he asked, shall we go on in a state of eternal war, or have peace amongst the different classes of society ? (Applause).

Mr. HENRY ENGLISH (President of the Political Union, and a member of the Amalgamated Society of Engineers,) said he should not occupy much of the time of his hearers, but on behalf of the Political Union and himself, he begged to thank Mr. Ward for his paper on the subject of " Capital and Labour," and also the Committee of the Literary Section of that Club for their kind invitation to the working classes, asking them to take part in the discussion, which was most important to all classes of society. Having had considerable opportunity of obtaining knowledge respecting the difference of the position between employers and employed, he did not consider that capital should, or ought to, take precedence of labour ; for it must be admitted that labour was the creator and producer of capital, and ever would be. That being the case, labour had a perfect right to assume power over capital, rather than otherwise. Labour carried on the face of itself the shining lucre for which all were more or less grasping so eagerly, and produced all that could be manufactured from the rude materials of the earth or the timbers of the forest. By its artistic hand, and the scientific development of the brain, it had fashioned the most ponderous design down to the most delicate taste, whilst it had shed abroad prosperity to our country, comfort in our homes, and peace in our land. Labour was the soul-stirring element of all true happiness, for whether we ride or walk, we are indebted to and dependent on the handicraft of the worker ; for if we look into the loftiest mansion or the humblest cottage, whether we stray into the workshop or dive into the bowels of the earth, we still must mingle with the labourer. Time would fail to enumerate the countless variety of designs into which labour was made to appear, and that was not necessary. He might be asked what part capital had to perform ? This seemed to be an easy task, assuming that money was capital. "The employer," said Mr. Ward, "must of necessity have anxiety, brainwork, knowledge, inventive genius, administrative skill, and a never-resting commercial activity. These are elements which must not—nay, cannot —be ignored." Here he would ask, how many of this standard could be found ? He did not deny that these were essential elements required to carry out the principle of business to a successful issue, but it did not absolutely follow that the employers should absolutely possess them, and it was a fact that two-thirds of the manufactories of England were carried on at this present time by managers, foremen, &c., whose brains, instead of their employers', became the prime movers in these gigantic works. He had known cases where managers had had thousands of pounds worth of work to superintend, and where employers knew not when it was begun nor when it was completed ; and if inquiries were made respecting it they were referred to the manager. Then it was not true that employers did, or must of necessity possess these qualifications, nor did they conduce equally in proportion to labour ; for labour was not only wasting its brain, but a man was through life wearing away his bones and sinews in the hope of that which he seldom realized. Could they ignore the fact that human strength was too sacred a commodity to be bought and sold, bartered away for a mere maintenance? Yet labour was asked to live on the smallest item of remuneration for the loss of vital existence. What would repay this loss ? They could not repay it with gold and silver. Labour could only be compensated by labour, because it demanded value received. Mr. Simons remarked that "Knowledge and Labour" would be more suitable than "Capital and Labour." He thought that gentleman could not have offered a greater insult to labour, for what constituted labour but intelligence and toil? (Hear, hear.) Was it not also true that men often started in a business of the secrets of which they were in total darkness? For if a man were in possession of a few hundred pounds, he might employ labour and brains which would carry forward his projects, even to exceed his own expectation; and that employers, as a rule, could not boast of their superior talent. They were told that capital was absolutely necessary to production. Granted it was so, but labour might do without the capitalist and become its own employer, thus disposing of a class of individuals whose claims far exceeded those of labour. If they took a deep view of the case, they found that as soon as labour commenced capital became the debtor until such time as labour became compensated. Capital, therefore, not only received labour as equivalent for capital, but the interest on capital due to labour, many firms holding fourteen and twenty-one days' wages in hand. This was an injustice, because they did not pay over to labour the banking interest, and therefore kept from labour its due, calmly pocketing the gains. Respecting piecework, there was something to be said in its favour, viewing it from a capitalist's point of view; for if piecework were taken, it naturally followed that men strained every nerve to produce to the fullest extent the greatest possible quantity of work. This was not done by labour alone, but by all the skill, energy, and intelligence possible for human power to devise. This having been done, the greatest facility is obtained, the largest quantity produced, and the highest amount of wages attained; but what followed? As soon as the employer detected the increased amounts earned, he asked the question how so much money was earned, whilst other workmen were not receiving more than half? The consequence was that the employer offers a less price, and the genius which had cleared the way and simplified the course must therefore accept it, or stand aside in idleness for the inferior workman, because of his inferior gains. Thus it would be seen that the employer had succeeded in extracting from the worker every grain of talent as well as labour, and was also enabled to place the inferior workman in his position, on account of the simplification of the mode of performing this certain calling, without the slightest reduction to the consumer of the article produced. The employer received the gains, and wages became lowered to a similar rate to day wages. Again, it was patent that in a brisk trade there was a surplus of labour, and by a regular system of piecework it must inevitably throw more out of employment; therefore, one would be toiling to the extreme to support another in compulsory idleness, and whilst such was the case capital would ever assert its power. He should be told that he did not consider the general benefit of the community, that he had no consideration for free trade, and that this mode of dealing would be the direct way to drive the trade into other channels. Well, let them see, and take example of the past. The following statistics were presented to both Houses of Parliament :—The entire exports of the United Kingdom for for the whole of the ten years ending 1772 amounted in value to £163,422,423, whilst for the year 1872 alone they amounted in value to £255,961,609, or upwards of ninety millions more in value for one year than during ten years a century ago. According to Mr. J. A. Mann, the entire exports of cotton goods in the year 1751 amounted in value only to £45,986, whilst in 1872 the value of cotton goods exported was £80,129,066. In the year 1770 the population of the United Kingdom was estimated at 11,198,276; in the year 1873 it was estimated to be 31,840,921 ; or, whilst our population has only doubled itself two and three-quarter times over our imports, which are an index to the growth of our national wealth, have increased twentyfold. As before stated, our total export of cotton goods in 1751 amounted only to £45,986. In 1872, notwithstanding the fact that cotton goods were at least five or six times as cheap as they were in 1751, they amounted to £80,129,066, or more than 1,700 times as much in value during the latter period as compared with the former ; whilst, if the estimate were in bulk, it would amount at least to eight or nine thousand times as much. For the year 1872 the entire value of our cotton manufactures was upwards of £90,000,000, whereas in 1757, as seen, they were only valued at £200,000. Or, to put it in another form, though our population has only increased about two and three-quartersfold, the yearly value of the cotton goods we produce has increased upwards of 450 fold, and if we make a calculation by bulk it will reach about 2,000 fold. With this immense increase of wealth in our midst who could say it was honest or just that one should accumulate a vast fortune in a short space

G

of time, which will enable him to roll and revel in luxury with a super-abundance of this world's treasures, whilst they who have toiled by hand and brain can scarcely eke out a miserable existence on the pittance doled out to them? And this was called compensation? One of the first solutions of this problem would be to adopt the noble example of some of the employers, for instance, Mr. Gimson, engineer, of Leicester, who was a large employer of labour. That gentleman stated, at a meeting which he was asked to address, that he firmly believed the time had come when something should be done to bring about a reconciliation between employers and employed. He had noticed with extreme pain the wide breach that now existed between the two parties, when it was of the highest importance that they should be bound together by the closest ties of friendship. He considered this, not only in a commercial sense, but from a social point, that it was the duty of every good citizen to use his best endeavours to aid in every form those means that would produce the greatest amount of happiness to the greatest number of people. (Hear, hear.) He had at that time set his idea into practice. He suggested to his workmen that he should be willing to accept a certain per centage for his capital, and the remainder of the profit should be divided according to their rate of wages ; that is, every man should receive equal per centage on the amount he obtained every half year. To this the men were not very unanimous, not knowing the working of these things. Ultimately, however, it was agreed to, and the first half-year they received five per cent. on their wages, and the second half-year six per cent., in all for the first year eleven per cent. In paying this dividend Mr. Gimson stated that he did not tor one moment suppose that he should realise so much gain as in previous years. His sole object was to cement the two parties together, and thus create that good feeling of fellowship which was so essential to the welfare of all mankind, but he was able to inform them that he had not only realised as much as on previous occasions, but his gains were in excess of any preceding year, and the workmen, to show that they were not slow to appreciate kindness, immediately set about a plan to show their gratitude for the good feeling and the generous spirit their employer had shown. In a short time they presented him with an address and a photograph, valued at thirty guineas. Thus it would be seen that this system of

working would have a threefold effect. First it would create a feeling
of responsibility, and an attachment to the employer which would prevent
many errors and accidents, and would stimulate them to despatch their
work upon the most improved principle. Secondly, it would make them
more honest, because a workman new that every drop of oil or piece of
iron, every portion of belt, and every kind of tool, as well as time, econo-
mised would be of so much benefit to him ; and if wasted, so much loss.
Thirdly, it would make men more industrious. They would be encouraged by the fact that whatever labour they performed, reward would
attend it ; and this would have the influence of removing the idler, because
if men saw their fellows taking the slightest advantage in any way, either
of time or material, they would meet them with the disapproval of the
whole establishment. This method would, therefore, have the effect of
producing the same amount as if on piecework, and as desired by Mr.
Ward ; each, too, would be benefited, and the prospects of the nation
enhanced. He would recommend the plan to all employers of labour, for
if it was not done quickly, to bring about a more amicable feeling between
contending parties, trades' unions would, without a doubt, become one
great national federation. This being once established, co-operation
would certainly follow, and then the vast amounts of capital would,
instead of being used to support men out of employ, be thrown into the
labour market, where it would receive the full benefit. And men,
instead of receiving pay from their unions, or money that had been used
to support compulsory idleness, would be contributing by their united
action to the augmentation of the fund and the prosperity of the society,
and thus in a short time would undoubtedly become a power that would
materially affect the large employers of labour in this country. It was
evident that the most intelligent, most honest, most industrious class of
individuals would be found in those societies, which would give an impetus
to their commerce ; whilst the careless, thoughtless, ignorant, and in-
different would be left outside for the use of private firms. He thanked
them for their patient hearing, and expressed the hope that great
good would follow these discussions, that the working classes might be
elevated, the employers made more happy, and that England might continue to grow in intelligence and commerce, and still hold her high place
amongst the nations of the earth. (Applause.)

Mr. COUNCILLOR GOLDSCHMIDT said whilst, like Henry IV. of France, he would like every working man to have his boiled chicken in his pot on the Sunday, he thought that even in the interests of labour it was necessary to say a word or two on behalf of capital. His working friends had had ample opportunity of ventilating this question which they were met to consider, and he must say that he was not prepared for the depth of the gap which existed between labour and capital as shown forth by these discussions. The question they were considering was, naturally, a very difficult one. It was difficult on account of the great principles which it involved—it was difficult on account of the different interests affected ; but it was particularly difficult on this account—that they could hardly approach it without bringing forward their grievances. (Hear, hear.) Now, if they could discuss it as one of broad and abstract principles, he thought they might better arrive at sound conclusions, and perhaps at some kind of solution. Supposing they first took the point as to the definition of capital, though he would not enter largely upon the matter of definition. Take capital to be an accumulation of savings, and he supposed they would also take it for granted that the law should protect those savings, which the savers might use for their own benefit if they liked, or for the benefit of those around. Mr. Smith, their Communistic friend had admitted that he would not by force take capital from the capitalist, but would in his own way create capital and neutralise the capital of the capitalist. Now, as to the theories of their Communistic friend, he thought they would be found to be neither new, nor ingenious, nor tangible, nor would they be for the benefit of humanity at large. Take, for instance, a community of a hundred thousand persons, who, on the Communistic principle, had to provide for themselves—that was to say, who had to live together, and eat, drink, and clothe themselves. He asked, how much interest had each of these hundred thousand persons in his own earnings or savings ? He had one hundred-thousandth part of benefit in his own earnings, or next to nothing. (Hear, hear.) Each man, being unable to lay by anything, and only having to satisfy the immediate cravings of hunger, or other immediate wants, would not try to do the most that he could—he would, on the contrary, do the least that he could, and leave the most that he could to his neighbour. (Hear, hear.) Consequently that community of 100,000 would not be enriched, but impoverished. If they had not to provide for more than the day in which they lived, they had not to provide for their children. But that community of 100,000 would eventually increase to 200,000 ; and whereas, in an ordinary state of society, among 100,000 persons they might have 10,000 who were well-to-do, and 90,000 who lived from hand to mouth, or from day to day, here they had to contrast what would be the general condition of the whole community. He should like to say to his friend Mr. Smith that it was quite right the Apostles lived in a state of communism. ("No.") Yes, it was quite right ; but it should be borne in mind that they represented to us that highest state of love which our own society generally does not represent. In the case of the Apostles they had that highest state of love, one living for the other ; whereas, in the ordinary condition of society we live, not one for another, but, unfortunately, every one for himself. In that happy state of society referred to by Mr. Smith, human nature would still be human nature. He would just briefly advert to those times, now long ago, when thousands emigrated from England to America, where, in various parts they founded Communistic States, or Communistic societies. And what was the result ? In 1610, he believed, when that Communism in Virginia was brought to a close, the people had arrived at beggary and ruin. But as soon as the rights of property were again established—as soon as every man could work for himself, one man did the work of three under Communism. If Mr. Smith wished to inform himself on the point, he would find this in the history of the United States, by Bancroft, part 1, page 161. He had put it down especially for that gentleman's benefit. This related more or less to all those States where the principle was introduced. He believed that in 1540, when the Anabaptists established in Germany a principle of the kind, after having consumed everything upon which they could lay their hands, they had recourse to great excesses. That society was hopelessly lost. These instances, he thought, though relating to remote history, might be a useful study to those Communists who imagined that from a Communistic system no end of advantage might be reaped. He wanted to refer to yet one more point. Louis Blanc, from whom Mr. Smith had learnt much, saw the difficulty of a Communistic system. He saw that it would lead to many abuses which were not common in ordinary society. As to each man having sufficient honour to do what was right in that Communislic society, and not having recourse to excess, he instanced military organization as a kind of Communism. Of course it was, but it should not be forgotten that in the military organization a variety of punishments had to be instituted. With the Anabaptists, too, severe punishments had to be resorted to, for men could not be got to do what was right according to law or morals. The next question, and one which ought not to be made light of, was as to capital. It was said that capital was produced by labour, and no doubt; and he was of opinion that if labour was careful, and provident, and wise, labour might accumulate much property. (Hear, hear.) No law forbade any man raising himself in the social scale. As it was said that in France each soldier carried in his knapsack the marshal's *baton*, so in England every working man had the opportunity of rising. (Applause.) Yet he must not expect to rise simply by declaiming against capital. Did they know what anxieties the capitalist had? A capitalist who was trying to do his duty was trying to provide for those whom he employed as much work as he could. (Hear, hear.) To do so he had to find a market for that which was produced, and he exerted himself generally at his own risk. If he failed, who was there to recompense him for his enterprise, and for the loss sustained by any risk which might have been run? No one, for he had to rely only upon himself. It must not be taken for granted that a man starting in business had only to put out his sign in order to make his fortune, as it was proved by statistics that out of 100 men 10 succeeded, while 20 are continually fighting a hard battle to struggle on, and 70 utterly failed. Looking at these facts in that light, capital certainly did not always rest upon a bed of roses. He quite agreed, however, that capital had its duties—that when the capitalist engaged in an enterprise involving the fortunes or interests of a number of workmen, he had his duties to the workmen. He certainly must take care that by greed, or avarice, he did not raise the price of his wares so that he could find no market for them. As Mr. Ward had said in his paper, also, if he disposed of inferior merchandise at a good price he committed a wrong, and this tended to throw the workmen out of employ. Again, who was to fix the amount of remuneration which capital was to have? (Hear, hear.) He had heard it said that 5 per cent. interest should be quite enough for the capitalist, but if they considered the question, could they think for a moment that 5 per cent. was sufficient remuneration for capital engaged in commercial enterprise ? Did they consider the risk a man incurred in buying, say machinery, which might in the course of a year or two be almost superseded ? Did they consider, also, the loss which a merchant suffered by bad trade, by mistaken speculations, and by panics of all kinds ? Capital wanted to be protected as much as labour, and he took it that capital was simply the engine which set the labour market in motion. It was true that an engine, though comparatively small, could nevertheless set in motion all the machines of a factory. Let them not, then, look on capital in such an insignificant manner. Let them not look upon it as hostile to labour, but as being the engine which set labour in motion, and as one which should be protected, and regarded by labour, so that it might not become injured. If, so to speak, they nursed and surrounded it as the sun which shone upon labour, he was sure that its rays would not go beyond labour, but would shine upon it and fructify it. (Applause.) As to labour, much had been shadowed forth on the subject, with a good deal of which he could agree. He should wish for every labourer to be well clothed, well fed, and well housed, and properly able to educate his children. (Applause.) Yet did labour always reap that which it ought ? Would every labourer, if he had his hand upon his heart, say that he had always made the best use of his money, and had spent it in a way beneficial to himself, his family, and society at large ? Nursing their grievances, and throwing them in the teeth of capital, would not do any good. What labour had to do was by combination, which already existed, to obtain for itself a proper position in its relations to capital ; but, that being obtained, to be satisfied, and not say, " We want a division of capital—we want not only what we can earn, but that which others have earned in times past." He did not think that fair or exactly English ; nor did he think that working men generally would endorse such a sentiment. Such a sentiment had only been uttered by one or two speakers from the other side of the house—(a laugh)—if he might use the expression. When unions where used for extortion or coercion they overstepped their proper position, injuring themselves as well as capital, and in this way, instead of being friends of society, became enemies. (Hear, hear.) He was glad to find that many of the speakers had disowned, on behalf of their unions, any inclination whatever to coercion. If capital and labour worked harmoniously together, each protecting the other—if labour would not nurse its dissatisfactions, but try to ameliorate its condition by fair and legitimate means—if the labourers would be frugal, prudent, and temperate, and foster that tendency towards education which, he was glad to say, had been taken up with so much spirit—(applause)—with respect to which he himself was a humble instrument, he was sure that in this manner labour would do what would benefit labour, and capital, and society. (Applause.)

Mr. E. KILLINGLEY (Honorary Secretary of the Literary Section of the Club) said, in reply to several speakers respecting the duration of the discussion, that an opportunity would be given for every gentleman to express his views fully and frankly upon the important subject before them, and that the termination of the debate would be for those present to decide. (Applause.)

Mr. MORRIS WOODHEAD (of the Independent Order of Engineers and Machinists), said that at the outset he wished, like other workmen who had preceded him, to thank the Committee of the Literary Section of that Club for the manner in which this discussion had been thrown open. The consideration of this subject was an important matter—not that he thought any sudden change would be brought about with regard to the relations between capital and labour, but he looked upon it as a step in the right direction. For his own part, he was inclined to the opinion that if local debates of this kind became fashionable throughout the country, a portion of the present incipient causes of strife between the two classes would be anticipated, or rather checked, and a great number of petty quarrels prevented. (Hear, hear.) Besides, when conflicts did take place, he thought they would be more easily and satisfactorily settled by both parties being more familiar with each other's motives and ideas. This subject had been discussed and considered almost from every point of view—from the capitalist down to the Communist—(laughter)—and they had had a highly-coloured picture from a non-union workman as to what he considered the peculiar hard-ships of his position. His idea of the position of a man who voluntarily excluded himself from a combination of his fellows was in such a case that it could not be maintained, perhaps, except from the most selfish considerations. On all hands they found that unions were admitted to be not only necessary, but, as far as the workmen were concerned, of considerable utility ; and it was never found that a non-unionist carried his opposition to union principles to the extent of declining to share in the benefits which undoubtedly resulted from the practice of those prin-ciples, his position being in fact that of a person who is willing to reap, yet declines to sow. His friend, to whom he referred, would probably reply that he did not consider it right that he should be called upon to become a member of any body with the principles and practices of which he might disagree. To such an excuse they could answer that for good or evil such institutions materially affected his welfare, and the welfare of those who were dependent upon him ; and if he saw those institutions doing what was detrimental to his interests he was open to the charge of moral cowardice in not offering to protect those interests. (Hear, hear.) There was one union, he found, which had almost escaped notice—the employers' union. He did not think that labour had anything to fear from combinations of capital, rather the reverse. The better disposed of the employers would hold in check the more unscrupulous, and the workmen, he believed, would always get as good terms, and a guarantee as to their fulfilment. There was one complaint as to the employers' union. It was that before the capitalists went into that line of business themselves, they used to hear a good deal about the laws of trades' unions. In his opinion the workmen had some reason to complain that they were entirely in the dark as to the laws and regulations of the em-ployers. (Hear, hear.) He was subject to correction, but so far as he was aware, no authenticated copy of their rules had ever come into the hands of the workmen. Were the employers jealous lest the workmen should copy the rules, and thus improve their own ? (Laughter.) At any rate, while the proceedings of the employers' association were con-ducted in so secret a manner they would be looked upon with much dis-trust by working men, and the action of those who were members of the association would generally have the very worst construction put upon it—

though sometimes unjustly, always naturally, under the circumstances. (Hear, hear.)   Whatever could be said about the institutions of the kind belonging to working men, they could at least claim the credit of being conducted in a more open way, not a few of them, in fact, submitting their rules to the scrutiny of a public official—the Registrar.   As to workmen's unions, he thought their worst advocates were those who contended that they were perfect, for such individuals stood in the way of improvement. (Hear, hear.)   At the risk of disagreeing with some, he must refer adversely to what, with unions, was known as the average rate of wages system.   He held that the practice of only allowing men to belong to the union who were able to obtain the average rate of wages in their town or district was unjust. (Applause.)   Members of a trade union not only sought to regulate, as far as they could, the price for which members should dispose of their labour, but they also did more. They gave the whole law and custom to the entire trade, and men who aspired to do that were bound to make their combination on such a foot-ing that all decent men in that trade should be considered. (Hear, hear.)   The rule adopted seemed to him absurd.   One object of unions was to maintain the standard of wages, but how was it to be done if they ignored the wages of the underpaid men, who required most look-ing after ? (Applause.)   This, as he thought improper, rule had its penalty.   In his own trade, the engineers, they had a union, of which they had already heard in the discussion—the Amalgamated Engineers —and no one was more ready to concede that so far as concerned the conduct of the business of that society, it was a model one, and com-prised thousands of men who, in point of intelligence and usefulness, were second to none in the world.   Nevertheless, it was founded on this average rate of wages system, and the moment it was called on to resist aggressive action on the part of the employers, or when it sought an advance for the benefit of the members, it not only had to contend with the opposing forces of capital, but also had to endure a dead-weight in the shape of non-union men.   This was chiefly owing to its own adherence to what he considered a very foolish and improper rule, which was in reality detrimental to the members themselves and to their interests. (Hear, hear.)   Take, for example, the case of a member who happened to have been brought up and so far followed his craft in a locality where a comparatively inferior class of work was done, say, for instance, agricultural machinery, and on falling out of employment, being anxious to extend his experience, he migrated to a locality—say Nottingham or Manchester—where he would be brought in contact with an entirely different and better kind of work than that to which he had been accustomed; under these circumstances it was not to be expected that he would be able to do an average quantity of that work, and the employer naturally declined to pay him the average wages. But the society must be consistent with itself, and as it refused to admit as members those who did not obtain the local average of wages, it could not permit its own members to work for less. The consequence was that this workman must either become obnoxious to his union or remove to some other place where he would find his own original class of work. He protested against anything that restrained a man from acquiring increased skill in his trade, and what is so likely to have that result as that which practically confines him to one particular style of work. (Applause.)

FIFTH NIGHT'S DISCUSSION.

(TUESDAY, MAY 12, 1874.)

MR. WOODHEAD (of the Independent Order of Engineers and Machinists), said that when the discussion was adjourned last week he was criticising a certain phase of unionism known as the average or minimum rate of wages system, and he should now only remark on this subject, that he considered associations formed on that principle were really aristocratic concerns, and the less the working classes had of that element amongst their institutions the better for those institutions, while at the same time they would be the more consistent in their criticisms of the aristocratic tendencies of other people's institutions. (Applause.) During the early part of this discussion he believed that some gentlemen expressed a preference for some other class of union, and he thought that this existed. It was established in Nottingham about two years ago, and he himself was one of the first members. In this union the restriction upon membership referred to a person's antecedents and present character —they did not draw the line as to the wages he was receiving. (Hear, hear,) If his wages were low, then he would go into a lower class of membership. This classification, though it might be characterised as of an aristocratic kind, formed an inducement to members to improve their position, and although the society had not been long established, men who had entered on a low rate of wages had proudly come forward and proclaimed their eligibility for a higher class of membership. (Applause.) This was partly owing to their own efforts and partly to the assistance derived from fellow members working in the same shop. In his opinion, this was a far superior class of unionism to anything that was possible under the other system to which he had alluded. (Hear, hear.) He was inclined to believe that it would be found to be the unionism of the future, and it encouraged that fraternal and mutual spirit between man and man which was so much to be desired. But while he freely admitted that trades' unions contained amongst them much which was anomalous, and even contradictory, he still thought, considering that until recently their whole class was in a state of almost compulsory ignorance, that they were entitled to congratulate themselves upon attaining so much good at the expense of so little that had been mischievous. (Hear, hear.) In other countries, with regard to such matters, there had been bloodshed and revolutionary strife, while England had quietly gone on until at length she stood by far the richest nation in the world ; and this was greatly due to the patient industry and orderly disposition of the working classes. What, he would ask, did these working classes wish for now ? As a working man himself—and he thought that in this matter he truly represented the sentiments of nineteen-twentieths of the English working men—he entirely repudiated any sympathy whatever with such mischievous nonsense as Communism. (Hear, hear, and laughter.) Those bugbears to society, leaders of trades' unions, about whom so much that was absurd had been written and spoken, did not wish, by means of such a character, to displace any of the wealth already acquired. (Hear, hear.) What they aimed at, and what they had a right to seek to attain in a lawful manner, was that the wealth of the future—to the production of which labour would of course continue to contribute—should be more fairly and equally distributed. (Applause.) He thought that every reasonable and thoughtful person would admit there was much room for improvement in this direction—in fact, in some quarters great changes were immediately inevitable. The farm labourer was no longer content to accept as his share of the rich harvests he toiled to produce the starvation wage of 8s. to 14s. per week, out of which he had to pay a large per centage for a miserable hovel which could afford him no comfort, and upon which less care and attention were bestowed than upon the landowner's dog kennel or a farmer's cowshed. (Applause.) Yet the land, which could afford him so little, was made to contribute immense resources for the purposes of that conceited specimen of humanity, the British landed aristocrat—(laughter)—and this, too, frequently in a career which was one of extravagant luxury. The previous speaker, Mr. Goldschmidt, with Mr. Ward in his paper, and several other gentlemen who had spoken, called their attention to the hard work, and the risks and anxiety of capital. A man would be really prejudiced and bigoted who denied that conductors of large industrial concerns, and capitalists generally, did not work exceedingly hard—in fact their work was sometimes of a more distressing character than that of the individual workman. (Hear, hear.) Nevertheless, they might look forward to the prospect of obtaining all the advantages which result from acquired wealth—a prospect which can scarcely be said to exist for the working man, no matter how hard he may work. Employers, too, no doubt, had frequently a very anxious time. When trade was slack, and when there was a panic or anything of the kind, employers had unquestionably to struggle hard in order to keep their capital and trade together. But, he asked, was their case more entitled to sympathy than that of thousands of working men, who had often to struggle hard, and sometimes to starve hard, in order to keep their homes together? (Hear, hear.) For himself, he did not think that it was. As to the risks of capital, certainly capital had large risks. Yet, could his hearers tell him of one in which labour did not fully share? In addition, had they no dangerous trades—no unhealthy occupations, and no cripples among them? And how many thousands of workers were yearly sent to their graves by accidental contingencies? As an illustration, it had been said that the capitalist might have his capital on board a ship, and the ship might be wrecked and the capital lost. But carry the illustration further. If the capitalist lost his capital, did not the sailor too frequently lose his life? And though, by insurance, the loss of the capitalist might be distributed over so large a surface that the individual loser was sometimes an actual gainer, they could not compensate for the widow's grief and loss, and who could compensate the sailor's child? (Applause.) If there was one thing which justified labour in seeking for itself something more than a bare subsistence, it was in order that those who laboured might be better able to meet the contingencies and risks that were inseparable from the lot of labour. (Hear, hear.) Mr. Goldschmidt asked whether, as a body, the working classes could lay their hand upon their heart and say that they had made the most of what they had. He was afraid they could not, as, for instance, the publican sometimes got a great deal too much. (Laughter.) Allowing, however, for all that could be said in this direction against his class, were there not still thousands of working men who from childhood had worked as hard, bodily and mentally, as any employer or capitalist, and who yet, in the autumn of life, found themselves cast off like old shoes, notwithstanding the prudence and frugality exercised by them, not having had the opportunity of accumulating sufficient to keep them from want and dependence in their old age ? (Hear, hear.) Mr. Goldschmidt asked whether the working classes were frugal. Now that was the kind of advice with which the working classes were familiar—(laughter)—and advice of which they frequently got a considerable quantity. To him it appeared that the advice was something after this fashion : supposing they caught a Scotchman, and, giving him a small quantity of oatmeal, left him on some barren and desert isle, saying, "Now, Sandy, be careful of what you have, as I shall not be back for a month "—(laughter)—it would be something on a par with such advice as that he had referred to As a class, he contended that working men knew well what frugality and carefulness were, having been taught in that best of all schools, experience, and under that sternest of teachers, necessity. (Hear, hear.) A charge against labour had been made in the course of the discussion as to which he should like to say a word or two. It was that working men had frequently resisted the introduction of new and improved machinery, and so forth. In the first place, he might remark that he considered that charge was somewhat out of date. He asked, would those gentlemen who made such a charge, give instances of recent occurrences of that kind ? Unless this were done, he considered that it was rather begging the question to reap up old grievances. (Hear, hear.) And when such things did occur, who was most to blame or most responsible ? Those who committed the folly through ignorance, or those who were responsible for that ignorance ? And did capital come into court, on this matter, with clean hands ? Let them ask such inventors as had introduced novelties, who would tell them that the greatest obstacles in their way had been those put there by people interested in the retention of old contrivances—capitalists themselves. (Hear, hear.) He thought that the less said on this subject by those representing capital, the better. He had next to allude to a matter which was rather a sore one as between capital and labour—piecework. He could not, in the first place, endorse the statement that piecework had been the ruin of every trade which had had anything to do with it. (Hear, hear.) If they would look round the country they would find that some of the largest and best paid industries were those in which piecework was the uniform rule. He might instance the mining trades, great portion of the Lancashire trades, and the Sheffield trades ; while, to come nearer home, there was the case of their friends the lacemakers. As a principle, he believed that piecework was incontestibly right, and to him it appeared that it simply applied to labour the same rules of exchange practised with regard to other commodities. (Hear, hear.) When a working man spent his wages, it was generally on the piecework principle—he required a stipulated quantity, of a certain quality, at a stipulated price. This principle had in its application the advantage that every worker could receive exactly in proportion to his ability and industry, so that he who had the most and best labour to sell got the greatest reward for it. (Applause.) But the question seemed to him to hinge almost entirely on the adaptability of this system to different classes of work, and also upon the use which employers made of it. In some trades no doubt there were great practical difficulties in the way. For instance, they could not send a man to repair a steam engine by piecework, and the same with a great many other things. In fact, the more complex a trade, the greater would be the difficulty. (Hear, hear.) He thought, however, that where an easy and simple measurement of work, in quantity or quality, could be found, piecework was right so far as principle was concerned. Although he fully admitted piecework to be right as a principle, he did not by any means concede that the resistance to it on the part of a great many working men was the result of either ignorance or prejudice. (Hear, hear.) In his own trade that of the engineers, they were in a very confused state in the matter, for in some towns the system flourished with the consent of all parties, while in others it was bitterly opposed. It might happen that a working man, who was a member, would be expected to leave his employment in one town rather than undertake piecework, and yet be sent to another town to work under the system as a matter of course. There could be no doubt that this was anomalous, and it was also awkward to all parties. It was not right that an employer in one town should be compelled to conduct his business differently from a similar employer in another town.

But who was to blame for this ? Though he conceded that the principle of piecework was right, he denied that working men resisted it on principle at all. It was the evil experience they had had of the misuse of a good principle by the employers themselves. (Hear, hear.) Supposing that an employer had a run upon a particular class of work, and that he wanted it to be done by piecework, he fixed a price, and one would almost think that, having all the materials for a proper calculation, he would fix on a price which he would be able and willing to adhere to. The piecework went on and, naturally enough, some workmen, by superior ability, might even double their previous wages, when it was generally found that the employer began to repent his bargain. (A laugh.) He said, "For those who were previously satisfied with 30s. a week to be getting £3 will not do, and as they will only spend it in drink, and as I have to carry on the concern, the money will be better in my pocket than theirs." (Laughter.) Upon that he dropped the price, say 10 per cent. Afterwards the thing came on again, until there was another step in the same direction, and thus the employer went on step by step, always fixing his standard by the best men, until, eventually, the average workman found himself worse off by piecework than he was formerly by day work, notwithstanding his increased hard labour. Employers not only liked to fix the price, but liked also to fix the limit of what a working man should be allowed to earn. It was an arrogant assumption on the part of capital, and one which every workman, whether unionist or non-unionist, must feel bound to resent. It might be summed up in this way—that when labour put on the steam, capital began to apply the screw ; and labour, naturally enough, declined to work continually at high pressure for people who were in a violent hurry to get rich. (Applause.) But he did not say at all that this statement of his referred to all employers. There were, no doubt, a great number who would willingly see their workmen earn as much as they could afford to pay them, no matter how much it might be. This, however, was one of those things in which, unfortunately, an unscrupulous few could direct the conduct of the. better-disposed. If one employer succeeded in getting his merchandise produced at a cheaper rate than another, so far as his labour was concerned, then he could undersell his more generous competitor in the market. It therefore arose that the

H

principle of piecework, which was so good in itself and so correct, was, in regard to many trades, so bitterly opposed. It was not on principle opposed, but the difficulty was the practice of it, and that difficulty was the old one, capital generally wanting more than its fair share. Mr. Ward, in his paper, called attention to what he termed the superiority of America to England in many respects, and as he (the speaker) had had some experience in the matter, he would venture to recount his ideas on the subject. In the first place, it was a mistake to suppose that the inventive power of which so much was heard with regard to America was due to any native superiority of the Americans themselves. (Hear, hear.) If they searched the records of the Patent Office in America, they would find that of the inventors a great number were natives of England or Germany—the larger portion of them—but who in their own country were content to go on from day to day in "I wish in my heart for Sunday" style. (Laughter.) In America, however, they seemed to have a new spirit and new energy infused into them by the democratic principles and customs of the country—they seemed, as it were, to breathe a different air. They went to work, and among their shopmates one, perhaps, had received a substantial reward for some little labour-saving contrivance, which in England would be passed over without notice; while in the case of another person, they might see him getting a considerable income beyond his wages, as profit out of some invention he had made. The men going there and seeing these things, began to try and do something for themselves — in fact, they went about the country like roaring lions, seeking for something to invent and improve. (Laughter.) And though he was ready to admit that out of every hundred who made the attempt ninety might fail, still the ninety were far better workmen for the attempt. (Applause.) This was how it came to pass that we have so many inventions from America—made, not entirely by the Americans, but very frequently by the slighted workmen who went from other countries. How was it in England? Could it be said that the laws of England on this subject were either democratic or just? Were they not rather made as though it were a truth that brains and money went hand in hand. (Hear, hear.) And yet how different was it! Why, if he were to recount the names of those who had been the founders of the great industries of this country, it would only be to recount the names of a number of working men. (Applause.) At a time like the present he need hardly remind his hearers of the example of the Scottish factory lad, David Livingstone, whose remains were so recently interred in Westminster Abbey, in order to illustrate that there were those among our working population who had in their minds everything it was possible for human nature to have which was good. (Hear, hear.) The laws of the country were not only very aristocratic on the subject of which he spoke, but so also were the customs. Employers in this country did not recognise the ingenuity of their workmen to the extent such ingenuity was recognised in America. Moreover, in England it was found, as a rule, that promotion in the workshop or factory did not go by merit. Generally, the man who got promoted was he who did most bowing and scraping in the office, and who could do the most "bullyragging" in the workshop. (Laughter.) Those were the men who, as a rule, obtained the best places. While on this matter, he would observe that he thought labour had great cause for complaint against capital. At different times there had been great efforts to alter the laws of this country as to patents, &c., or all the laws bearing upon this important question. He should like to know how it was that those efforts had so invariably failed. It could not be said that the working men stood in the way, for they, and especially unionists, had been anxiously waiting to see those things placed upon a right footing ; and it could not be stated that the interests of the community were in the way, for the reverse was generally the case. Who was it, then, that had stood in the way ? In the opinion of his own class, it was capital and the monied classes generally. But whoever it might be standing in the way, there need be no mistake on this point—that until some reform took place in the matter it would be in vain for them to build, and try to drive their workmen into, technical schools. They would not go to school, and they were not likely to learn the technicalities of their respective trades when, having succeeded in improving anything, they found that they would have to contend against the obstructions in the way of achieving a proper and legitimate reward. (Hear, hear.) They would have to take that lock off the door of our Patent Office which effectually prevented the admission of any but those who were fortunate enough to possess a golden key. (Laughter and applause.) But when these things

were done—when reform in these matters took place, so that a real protection for the products of their ingenuity was afforded to rich and poor
alike—it would be found that England would not at all lag behind in
the race. (Hear, hear.) When those laws to which he had referred
were altered and suitably amended—when education had done its
beneficent work—when co-operation had reduced the monopoly of large
capitalists, it would be found that working men would learn their trade,
and the technicalities of it, themselves ; while the dormant, latent, and
at present despised mental energies so abundant in our working classes
would be brought to bear fully on the magnificently rich and conveniently
concentrated natural resources of our country. (Hear, hear.) When
that was done, England would assume her proper position at the head of
the industrial world—she would assume, rather, the first position in
the industrial world—a position which was hers not only by virtue of
her present acquired wealth, but which was hers by the power of her
people to cater even more successfully in the future than in the past for
the comforts, necessities, and luxuries of mankind. (Loud applause.)

Mr. JOHN CROUSE said that when he first entered that room he
came more as a listener than with the object of speaking. But now,
having attended every meeting which there had been in this matter, he
felt it to be his duty to say a word or two upon the question. Like
several other working men who had spoken, he was thankful and
gratified that Mr. Ward's excellent paper should have been brought
forward in such a way, and he was also pleased at the discussion which
had taken place with respect to it. It had for a long time been the
opinion of himself, as well as of a large number of others, that the question was one deserving to be carefully considered and discussed in all
companies, in order to ascertain, if possible, whether a better understanding could not be come to between capital and labour. (Hear, hear.)
He wished to remark that he objected to the reference made by a
previous speaker, Mr. Hancock, to the workmen of one of the staple
trades of the town—the lace trade—to which he himself belonged. That
gentleman had stated that a twisthand had admitted to him that five out
of six men with whom he had worked were not worth their salt. With
such a remark he (the speaker) could not agree, and he would like to

ask whether the same observation would not also apply to a large number of employers, as men ?   Mr. Ward, in his paper, said that "In England capital, pure and simple, receives a less amount of interest than in any other country."   He believed that, as a rule, working men were perfectly ready to admit the truth of this, and they had always done so ; but when that capital was combined with labour, it received more in return in England, if properly applied, than in any other country.   But he should say that the working classes did not get their fair share..   Mr. Ward further said, " I know that individual liberty has often been trampled in the dust, and the most cruel coercion exercised in the interests of trade unions, and they must therefore not complain if it be sought to keep them [to their just and proper influence, and within the bounds of what is fair and right."   As to this, he would admit that there had been errors on the part of trades' unionists at various times, but he should also like an admission that in the past there had been errors on the part of capital.   He (the speaker) believed there were a number of employers in the lace trade who did not like their men to belong to the co-operative society in the trade.   In conclusion, he stated that he should like the Masters' Association to take their laws, rules, and regulations before the Registrar, in order that they might in this way be duly signed and certified, or, otherwise, scratched out. (Laughter and applause.)

Mr. W. H. STEVENSON (Articled Clerks' Society) said that, like a previous speaker, he might offer a few observations as a comparatively disinterested spectator.   He should not have wished to say anything but that, as it was sometimes said, onlookers usually saw most of the game.   As to something which had already been advanced, if the only grievance working men had was that capitalists obtained an undue share of profit, when men worked for capitalists they were presumably satisfied with the wages given.   Those who took the side of labour could not argue as though one particular rate of wages was just, and those who did not pay it defrauded them, for it seemed to him that labour was worth just so much as it would fetch.   (Applause.)   They must admit, on the part of the workman, that the capitalist was under no obligation to employ him ; and the masters must admit, on their part, that the workmen were under no obligation to work for them. This, he thought, should be borne in mind. As to a minimum rate of wages, some, on the part of capital, appeared to think that they were injured by it. But supposing there was a certain amount of money which the masters were content to spend in wages to their workmen, if the workmen liked to say, "Instead of one-half getting 30s. a week and the other half only 20s., we will fix the rate at 25s. generally," they had quite a right, on their part, to submit these terms to the masters. He was not inclined to think that the masters could complain of the workmen having a minimum rate of wages. Some of the gentlemen who had spoken seemed to think it coercion on the part of unionists to refuse to work with non-union men, but surely this was a question for themselves. In the exercise of their undoubted right they said, "We prefer not to work with people who refuse to join our society." If workmen thought it better that all should be members of the society, they had a right to say that they did not care to give their labour to those masters who did not employ working men belonging to their society. So, he thought, they might go through many of the questions raised by Mr. Ward's paper. It had been endeavoured to be shown that the interests of both masters and men lay in the same direction, but it should be borne in mind that the rate of profit was variable. So long as our present system of property continued, it seemed to him that there must be these struggles between capital and labour. The only thing they could hope to do was by such meetings as the present, and by an increased knowledge on the part of both classes, to lessen the bitterness of the strife when it took place; make contention as short as possible where it was brought about, and have it less bitter than had been the case in the past. Communism, with which one speaker had dealt, had never been found to work. He should almost have liked that gentleman to have told them for whose benefit he proposed to introduce the principle of Communism. Its use to persons who were unable to take care of themselves had been attempted to be shown, and it had been argued that, at present, often those who invented what was of the greatest use to the nation received very little return. Communism was the remedy suggested, under which, whereas now such persons got little, the effect of the alteration proposed would be that they would get nothing. (Laughter, and "No, no," from

Mr. Thomas Smith). He would add that if he had not advanced much which was worth hearing, he was satisfied if he had raised a few points that were worthy of being discussed. (Applause.)

After an explanatory observation from Mr. ELSEY, in reply to Mr. Crouse,

Mr. THOMAS BLOOM stated that, in acknowledgment of what had been stated by several non-members as to the action of the Literary Section of that Club, he thought it should be said that it had afforded not only the members of the Committee, but also the members of the whole Club, the greatest pleasure and satisfaction to see the large attendance of those who had come especially to represent labour as against capital at these meetings. In addition, it had afforded the members generally considerable—he might say unexpected—pleasure to find that the views of those who had been invited were so ably and forcibly put forward from time to time, together with what they conceived to be their interests. Personally, after much thought, he was bound to come to this conclusion—that trades' unionism, throughout the land, had been caused in days past by the grasping and grinding spirit of certain masters in all trades. (Hear, hear.) He had weighed the matter over very carefully in his own mind, and, though a capitalist himself, he nevertheless felt, in looking at the past, that the masters had themselves to thank for the evils of trades' unions, and he thought there were evils even at present. He felt that they would have to bear with those evils. however, for it was only the rebound from a sense of the injustice done in days gone by. Supposing they went back to the history of England for about two hundred years, they would see the utmost licentiousness in religion and other matters rampant. The fact aroused the determination of the really earnest and thinking men of the day to intense action against this state of things, and the action to which he had referred brought forth the opposite of that licentiousness—a body of men for whom he should always feel the greatest reverence, the Puritans of England. (Hear, hear.) As to this subject of capital and labour, under the whole of the circumstances, they could not expect perfection on the part of labour. He believed that trades' unions, properly conducted,

would be of great and even immense benefit, not to one class alone, but
to the community at large. He had seen with sorrow that there had
been serious errors committed, but he hoped that the representatives of
labour would recognise the errors of the past, and, reasoning with
capitalists at such meetings as the present, see if some good could not be
quietly done, instead of going in for brute force either one way or the
other. (Hear, hear.) He felt sure that with unions conducted upon a
right and proper basis, labour would get its fair and suitable reward, and
he was sure that employers of labour, and capitalists generally, would
also get their fair share of reward. But if the trades' unions of England combined to raise wages to an abnormal point, then the manufacturers must raise their prices, and trades' unions must be careful lest
they drive the trade from this country. This point was forcibly brought
to his mind last week, in Manchester, when talking to several manufacturers. The only one who stood up boldly against trades' unions was
one from the north of England, the others saying that they were glad of
unions which were well conducted, and so long as they were on a sound
and fair basis. (Hear, hear.) One gentleman, a large manufacturer
in the woollen trade, said that so long as he could compete with the
manufactures brought against him, the higher the rate of wages he paid,
the greater were his profits and the greater his satisfaction. But
another gentleman instanced the case of his father-in-law, who, he said,
bought a tremendous quantity of iron during the year, and who had been
compelled to desist from giving orders to a firm with which he had been
in the habit of dealing very largely because he could buy iron, and did
so only last week, at £2 per ton lower than in England. The matter
being argued, the conclusion was arrived at that the fact was due to the
great increase in the prices paid for obtaining coal and iron. (Hear,
hear.) He thought that the rates for getting these commodities had gone
on to an abnormal and to an unnatural extent. (Hear, hear.) So,
while trades' unionists stood up for their right, which he held they had,
of obtaining a fair day's pay for a fair day's labour, they must not forget
that the capitalists of England ought not to be weighted down until they
were unable to successfully compete abroad. He hoped they would
have more meetings like the present, for he was sure that the result
could only be good, both for masters and men. The capitalist might

come forward and say, "You have made me a boot which fits very badly," but the representative of labour might point out that the cause of complaint was a corn that required to be cut. (Laughter.) He was very much pleased that a large manufacturer, and a member of that club, Mr. W. G. Ward, should have come forward in such a manner, believing that both the representatives of capital and labour were also gratified. He again hoped that there would be more meetings like the present, and that the interests of labour would be advanced with as much ability on those occasions as during this discussion. Before sitting down, he would again acknowledge the complimentary remarks made as to the action adopted by the Literary Section of that Club. (Applause.)

Mr. JAMES J. P. KIRK said certain speakers on the workmen's side had objected to Mr. Simons's new name for this discussion, "Knowledge and Labour," and on the part of those who were neither capitalists nor workmen he himself would do the same. He was unable to conceive what Mr. Simons could mean. Did he mean that all the knowledge was arranged on the side of capital against labour? He should say nay to that. Or was merely technical knowledge meant? Even in that case the title was not well chosen, for technical knowledge was as necessary to the workman as the capitalist. He imagined that outsiders hearing of a discussion on "Knowledge and Labour," would be at a loss to understand what was intended. They would perhaps fancy it was some debate on the superiority of knowing Greek or making a ditch. As to the subject of Communism, it had not been met in an altogether fair manner by the several speakers. It was no disproof at all of the system to say that because in certain cases it had failed, it would fail here, under other circumstances, in an old established country like our own, where there was not such a struggle for life as formerly in the American colonies. If they took the necessary produce of the world, he thought it would be found that it was just about sufficient for man's comfort. A comparatively small portion had a great superabundance, while with a great number there was a small deficiency. This was under the present state things, when the fear of poverty urged every man on to labour; but how under Mr. Smith's administration? Every man would have as little inducement as possible to labour, and they would find the produce of man's labour continually decreasing, until, at length there was not sufficient for his comfort, nor even for his existence ; and the force of circumstances would compel a return to the former state of things. But there was another and, to his mind, more incontrovertible argument against this theory. The greater part of men had very little education beyond what they gathered in the hard struggle of life ; default in that education of life nothing could remedy, except the highest culture, which comparatively few would be able to obtain. It would be a great mischance if the principle of self-reliance—of each man's trust in his own exertions—were taken away. Each relying on the Government, would work as little as he could for the community, for which he cared little, and which to him could be little more than an idea. They would become depraved, like the Hindoos and other eastern nations reared under the fostering care of a paternal Government ; and it would soon be found that loss of self-reliance was also loss of liberty. They would fall an easy prey to other countries by their habits of daily life reared to greater hardihood. It would be a sad day for England when her working men, losing their trust in their own right hands, should rely for subsistence on any Government, whether paternal or Communist. (Hear, hear.)

Mr. LOUIS SIMONS said he rose at this point in self-defence—(laughter)—and he had no doubt that his hearers would readily grant him the privilege. On the first evening of the discussion he said, as to the paper read by Mr. Ward, that if even the title "Capital and Labour" were well understood and used in all countries, not only in England, he would not object to it, though he did not think, nevertheless, that the title was a thoroughly good one ; and he added that he would rather say, "Knowledge and Labour," because capital alone, without knowledge, would not be able to achieve that which capital and knowledge would do. (Hear, hear.) It was a fact that he had said something at the same time, in reply to a gentleman who had spoken before him, about coercion on the part of union leaders. His remarks had been given in the most friendly spirit. He meant to say that "Knowledge and Labour" was a better title, for "capital" created jealousy and unfriendly feeling, while "knowledge" was a more friendly word, and could be acquired by every one. (Applause.) He did not say, and certainly did not think, that the working classes had no knowledge, or did not require it, or could do without it. He scarcely thought that he himself would have a workman without knowledge, and he thanked God that he had not one. (Applause.) He might boast that he had some very clever men, and they lived very friendly together. Fault had, nevertheless, been found with him by unionist and Communist, and, indeed, by nearly every one. (Laughter.) The knowledge of working men, he held, had made England what she is. Looking at Manchester, Belper, Leeds, and other places, need he give them names? He thought not. Then let them look at the spinning and weaving machines. In our own town of Nottingham, need he give them the names of those who, though they had worked at the frames, made fortunes before they died? His hearers should know those matters better than he, who only came to the town twenty or thirty years ago. Or should he remind them of the case of Mr. George Elliott, who had worked himself up to be a Member of Parliament? That was what he had meant by "Knowledge and Labour," and he was sorry that he should have been misunderstood. He was very glad to find that all union men were not of the same opinions, as they had found in the course of the discussion; and, in conclusion, he would state that he had listened to the remarks of Mr. Woodhead on that occasion with much pleasure. (Applause.)

Mr. FRANK PARKER said that a previous speaker had seemed to be labouring under the impression that trade was about to be driven out of the country, owing to certain classes of workmen demanding an extortionate price for their labour. He maintained that those particular workmen alluded to had not demanded the price for their labour which many persons seemed to be under the impression that they had demanded, and that it was not they, but capitalists, who had been at the root of all the evil. Referring to the miners, and taking four or five years ago, not only in this district, but in others in the Midland Counties where coal was obtained, the price of the best coal was about 13s. per ton. Since that time wages had gone up, but he did not think that if the kingdom were searched through, it would be found that miners' wages had gone up more than say 1s. or 1s. 6d. per ton for the getting. Here was the fact before them. But a few months ago, however, they were

paying as much as 25s. and 26s. a ton for almost anything in the shape
of coal that was fit to burn. He should like to know then how the
excessive prices had been created, and who had created them? Who,
he asked, were to blame? and was it the miners? He thought they had
now before them clearly enough that the capitalists had derived the
profit, and had put it into their coffers, while thousands of poor persons,
during the cold weather, had not had sufficient coal with which to keep
themselves warm. The impression which had very generally circulated that the fault lay with the workmen was, therefore, an error, and
he considered that there should be an end of the matter so far as
regarded them. Many seemed to be under the conviction that it was the
miners, and they only, who had been the cause of the excessive high
prices of coal, by demanding extortionate wages ; but he did not think
so, believing that capital, and capital alone, was to blame. (Hear, hear.)
The question of piecework had been touched upon by various speakers,
and he should like to offer one or two observations on this point. He
agreed very much with what had been said on the subject by Mr.
Woodhead, so far as that gentleman went ; but he thought that he was
in a position to go even further. Mr. Woodhead said the system was all
very well in certain branches of trade, where it was a straightforward,
go-ahead business, in which the work required to be done might be
executed with something like facility ; but that there were certain other
branches of trade which did not come under the same category. He
believed that piecework was a great evil in many respects. Put a
man into an ironfounder's shop, who was a first-class man at his
trade, and well-skilled in his business, but who was yet of little
intelligence, in other things — a man of no sound principle whatever,
though he excelled in that particular branch of trade to which
he belonged. This man being placed in a certain shop, let them
imagine him put to piecework. After agreeing to work under that
system, a bargain was struck with the employer as to the terms upon
which the work was to be done, and the man started. He went on
working for a time, doubling and perhaps trebling his previous wages,
owing to his extraordinary skill. That work being finished was passed,
and presently other work came to the man, which was also disposed of. But
shortly afterwards a similar class of work to the first was brought, though,

unfortunately not upon the same terms, a reduction being made. The master, seeing that under the original agreement the man made more money than he cared for him to make, and, thinking that the man had no right, effected this reduction. That was surely not at all right, for if a man had superior ability he ought surely to be paid for it when that ability was exercised. (Hear, hear.) Again, the work-man referred to, with scarcely any good principle in him, but with much of the talent or ability of his trade at his fingers' ends, could sweep ahead of his fellows, who perhaps happened to be far better men in numerous other respects, although not so expert in that particular branch of trade; yet this man, taking a job by piecework, laboured to such an extent that he had the effect of lowering the price of wages, the master regulating generally according to the man's ability, and the second-class workman had to follow in the footsteps of the first-class, until eventually it came about that a man who occupied a position in the middle or moderate class of workmen was scarcely able to obtain a bare subsistence. (Hear, hear.) In this case, he was inclined to think, there could be no difference of opinion as to whether or not piecework was injurious, and as to whether it was often a great evil to those who were employed. He might here just observe that it was his own parti-cular branch of trade that he was trying to illustrate. He believed that piecework was an evil, and he was of opinion that in opposing it he would be doing a service to himself and to many others; for in his own class of business there were many men who did not study what was really sound principle, and he was sorry that in too many cases drink was at the bottom of it. Nevertheless, there were very many others who were good, honest, industrious, and intelligent men. He thought that piecework would be better abolished altogether. There might not be so much objection to the system as now, if it could only be carried out upon a proper footing—if they could have something like a sound basis to work upon; but when employers would take an advantage where it was to be had, and would not adhere to a bargain, surely it behoved a man to look, not only as far as he could reach, but before him—not only at what he himself was going to have at the present, but at the future. (Applause.)

SIXTH NIGHT'S DISCUSSION.

(TUESDAY, MAY 19, 1874.)

MR. W. P. HEMM (of the Independent Order of Engineers and Machinists,) said that the subject under discussion had been well ventilated up to the present time, and he doubted not that both capitalists and workmen would have better understood the subject from the manner in which it had been placed before them. And there was no doubt that the subject was one of the most important which could occupy attention. He was satisfied that it was the all-in-all, so far as this world was concerned, with the working classes. It had been stated by some of the previous speakers that the working classes were not so frugal as they might be — that they did not take proper care of the pounds, shillings, and pence which came into their possession. Now, he took it that such a charge was not simply to be applied to one party, for his firm conviction was that in this matter it was applicable to both sides; and it was found that there were men among the capitalists, who, having realised large sums of money, allowed them to slip through their fingers. Before proceeding further, however, he must join in the commendation expressed by many speakers as to the paper itself. Taking it altogether, it was a very fair estimate of labour and capital, though there were portions of it which he should have liked to hear more fully illustrated. For instance, the paper dwelt somewhat largely upon the faults of trades' unionists—very largely upon labour, but very little upon capital. (Hear, hear.) He could not say whether this was because capital was exempt from any failings in the estimation of the reader of the paper, or whether because it was thought that these failings were rather within the province of the working classes to consider and discuss. Yet, altogether, he must look upon the paper as an excellent *résumé* of the subject. To revert to an observation he had already made, they had several times been told that the working classes were not frugal ; but it was a mistake. Very frequently they exercised greater economy than those who occupied positions above them. Those who had not mixed with them did not, and could not be expected to, understand the mode in which many of the working classes dispensed their funds. He once worked for a very large firm in Lancashire — Messrs. Sharpe, Roberts, and Company, the great engine manufacturers. He recollected a remark made after he left that place by his then employer. This gentleman said it was of no use giving workmen large wages, for they did not take care of that which they earned, the common practice being to spend a large proportion of it in the public-house. Further, he said that Mr. John Sharpe had made the remark to him that if he went round the works of his (Mr. Sharpe's) firm on the Monday morning, the men having received their wages on the previous Saturday, scarcely one would be found who had half-a-crown left. To this he (the speaker) replied that if there was a man who had half-a-crown left, probably it would be the man who was in the habit of spending his money continually, but who on that particular occasion had taken care of it, for working men generally calculated, on the week, the amount of money they were to receive, and the manner in which they were to expend it. After paying so much for house rent, so much for food and clothing, so much for the savings' bank, and so much for clubs, there was very little left for their pockets. (Hear, hear.) They had been told repeatedly, by some of the speakers, that trades' unions were not good things ; but he must give Mr. Ward credit for having said that he believed all should unite, both employers and employed. He wanted to show them what was done by large numbers of the working classes, and would endeavour to prove that they were more frugal than they had been given credit for. In the first place they paid, week by week, a sum of money which was collected into a fund, and after it was collected into this fund it was dispensed in a manner which he would attempt to explain. Supposing that room to be the club-room, and a man had to answer before his club-mates how it was that he had been discharged. If it was in consequence of any bad act on his part he was not allowed any benefit—or, rather, what was termed donation, which was so much a week to keep him whilst out of employment. In such a case he had to pass through this ordeal before he could receive benefit from the society to which he had been weekly paying. Mr. Ward expressed the opinion that unions should have that kind of funds, and he wished that gentleman to understand that they had them. A man would receive donation money for the whole of the year, because out of employment—not because there had been a strike ; for the rules of many of the unions, as now existing, did not recognise strikes. So it would be seen that wherever a strike occurred subscriptions had to be made round the different works. Or some of the unions might have what was termed a benevolent fund—an extra fund to which the members subscribed, and which they voted away in certain sums, as they thought fit, for those who were discharged or turned out. If an individual met with an accident when following his employment, if that accident were serious he was allowed £100 out of the funds to enable him to start in some little kind of business. Surely that was a good thing, both for the person who suffered by the accident and for the State. (Hear, hear.) As to the question of superannuation, provision was made for this. When a man became aged, infirm, and unable to work, he was allowed so much a week from the fund for this purpose, and, in addition, he might earn a further sum, so that it should not exceed, together with his allowance, a certain amount. Provision was also made in case of death, and, therefore, in these departments they were right. In the case of joiners, and similar persons, who were liable to the loss of tools from fire or some other mishap, when this occurred the society to which the individual belonged provided him with fresh tools in order that he might continue to follow his employment. There were but few societies which provided for the emigration of members, and had that as one of their objects, though they did pay money to enable members to migrate from one part of the country to another to procure employment. He thought that both employers and workmen present would understand that this was a most excellent arrangement on the part of unions, and one which was to the advantage of both parties. (Hear, hear.) There was one thing which he had not named, and it was a benefit of a different kind. He referred to what was called the " vacant book," and this applied to most trades. He would endeavour to explain the manner of its use, as well as its object. A book was kept at the club-house

in which the names of those persons who were out of employment were inserted, and generally the description of work which they
were accustomed to perform. Supposing an employer wanted a man to
do a particular kind of work, the men working for that employer soon
knew of the fact. The master was anxious to be suited, and sometimes
they would see an advertisement in the paper. Most unionists, when
they saw such an advertisement for a man, were inclined to think that it
was a bad place, and that the employer was changing very frequently,
considering that trades' unions were so anxious for their men to be
employed. (A laugh.) This "vacant book" was kept for the entry of
names of persons out of employ, with the department of the trade to
which they were most accustomed. It was the duty of members knowing that a man was wanted to go to the "vacant book," or, rather, to its
keeper, and inform him of the vacancy; and the first man suitable for
the position was ordered out to seek the person who wanted such a man.
This system was an advantage both to the employer and to the employed,
bringing the two together who wished to meet. (Hear, hear.) Supposing, to speak of another matter, that an employer had under him a
good workman who was a non-unionist, and this person wanted to join
the union. The first question asked at the meeting of the society was
what amount of wages he received, and whether he obtained what was
called the average rate of wages. If he did not, with regard to some of
the societies he would not be admitted, while, with regard to others, he
would be admitted, though under a certain classification. The next
question was, "What sort of a man is he?" and there was full inquiry
as to his character. According to the character detailed to the meeting
—and it was written down—he was admitted or rejected. With such
regulations, it should be expected that trades' unions would have within
their ranks the cream of their respective trades. They would have as
their members the best men in those trades, for they would not receive a
disreputable person if they knew it. Yet it was possible for a person to
be admitted who was not up to the mark, and he thought his hearers
would acknowledge that black sheep found their way into almost every
society. In the union, however, if they did anything that was wrong,
they were liable to be bowled out, while, if they retained a good and
proper position in the organisation, they found it ultimately to their

I

advantage. Employers had often to pay largely to the rates in order to
support those who were wanting employment, and working men had to
do so in like manner. But, by frugality and care exercised with the
funds appropriated in the manner he had attempted to describe, they
saved the rates, and felt that they were freeborn Englishmen, without
being paupers on the parish, when work was scarce and their trade was
giving them support. (Applause.) Was it not a good thing for them
all ? He maintained that it was, and also, that a man felt most independent who had provided for himself when out of employment.
Another remark or two as to this matter. There were some people who
occasionally made errors, and he was sorry that Mr. Hart should have
made one the other night. That gentleman said that whilst poverty
existed as a principle among us, neither combination or trades' unions,
nor anything else, could be of much avail in the matter. (Hear, hear.)
Now, he thought that he had been able to show his hearers that trades'
unions and combinations of labour were of much avail. They had
mitigated, to a considerable extent, the evils of poverty, and in many
cases men with large families had been prevented from becoming what
Mr. Hart had described as paupers not merely of to-day. He maintained
that, from the operation of unions, the evils of poverty had been to some
degree mitigated, and were continually being mitigated If so, then, they
were doing something which was to the advantage of society.

Mr. HART wished to be allowed to explain that he had not used the
word pauper in application to trades' unionists at all. Before he spoke
Mr. Start had said that there were a million of paupers and a million of
thieves, and he believed that Mr. Albert Richards made a similar statement. He did not wish it to be supposed, for a moment, that he had
designated trades' unionists paupers.

Mr. HEMM continued that he had not said this of Mr. Hart, and he
supposed that that gentleman had misunderstood the manner in which he
had expressed himself. He wanted his hearers to understand that, as a
class, trades' unionists produced few paupers in comparison with other
classes. Mr. Woodhead spoke very distinctly and clearly, in the preceding week, on the subject of piecework. (Hear, hear.) It was fair to
say that he (the speaker) believed piecework to be the proper principle

upon which trade should be carried on as between employers and employed, but there were to be taken into consideration the difficulties by
which they had found the system to be surrounded. He was not a
young man, and from the experience he had had, must have some knowledge of the manner in which the piecework principle was conducted.
In reference to his own trade, he would state that it was conducted
differently in different localities. In Lancashire, for instance, the price
of the work being fixed, the workman, who was sometimes considered to
be stupid, would work hard and long until, at the end of a week, or it
might be six weeks, on taking a reckoning he discovered that he had
earned rather more in consequence of having exercised, in such a way,
his skill and energy—realising, perhaps, rather more than what was
known as time and a quarter. But in stepped his master, and, not
allowing for the extraordinary ability which the man might have, took
so much per cent. off. In another establishment probably it would be
time and a third, and here, in a similar case, the same line of action was
adopted. Under these circumstances, what was there to induce a man
to work additionally hard when he knew ultimately his remuneration
would come down lower than before ? (Hear, hear.) These were the
sort of things which caused working men to say that they did not like
piecework. If the system were carried on properly, he agreed with his
friend Mr. Woodhead that it was a just and proper principle, and one
which they should all cultivate ; but not with the idea that if a man
with unusual ability made more than what was known as time and a
quarter or time and a third, he must be cropped down. (Hear, hear.)
There were, with employers, honourable exceptions, where an undue
advantage would not be desired, but these employers were compelled to
give way through the unscrupulous, especially in his own department of
trade. Something had been said, in the debate, as to strikes and lock-
outs. He thought that everything which was possible should be done to
prevent strikes, which, he was sure, were disadvantageous to both employer and employed. (Hear, hear.) And then, he had paid a considerable amount of money to men out of employment, because they were
locked out. In one trade to which he belonged no less a sum than
£52,000 had been paid in one strike. (A Voice : "It shows the men
get stunning good wages," and a laugh.) Well, the men did not get so

much as the lacemakers, and he for one was sorry that they did not. He believed in something other than a strike, which was a consuming fire that destroyed everything and did no good to anything. (Hear, hear.) A strike was one of the last things in the world which woiking men should enter into. Besides, the employers' capital was thereby wasted, lying unproductive ; and then there was the angry feeling which arose, as well as the exhausting of the men's funds. He wished it to be understood that great economy was exercised in strikes. Large amounts were not paid away, and he had known men to go on 5s. a week each, not taking the family a man might have into account. Upon this they had lived, or, rather, existed. He believed that they should endeavour to adopt a plan which would do away with these strikes—these lock-outs—these turn-outs, and one by which they might come at a more friendly way of settling differences which arose. The other night Mr. Goldschmidt said that the gulf between the two classes was a very deep one, and if they could get a bridge over that gulf they would have accomplished something worth accomplishing. (Hear, hear.) He approved of the principle of co-operation, which was mentioned by Mr. Ward. He himself was a co-operator—he had been one almost from a boy, and he believed he should continue to be one until he had passed to his last home. Co-operation, he considered, was the principle which would settle all these disputes, and it only wanted carrying properly into effect. At present it was partially carried out, but only partially. Yet it could be done, and with a proper amount of interest to capital, which should be fairly dealt by. If, under the system, there was any loss, it would be spread over the capitalist and the men who worked, in proportion. In Manchester the workpeople at a cotton-spinning place wanted an advance of wages, and asked for it. The spinner said that he could not afford the advance, as the profits from the business were not so great ; but the workpeople did not turn out, though they were threatened with being locked out if they were not satisfied. In the following week a balance-sheet was printed of a manufacturing co-operative society in Oldham, showing that large profits had been realised, at the same time that the other concern was not able to give the advance. This stopped any locking-out, and the employer met his workpeople half way, which, he believed, prevented any further dispute.

He thought he had said sufficient to show that under these co-operative manufacturing concerns of which he had spoken capital would get proper interest, labour its fair share of profit, and the purchaser a fair bargain for the money he paid. As to improvements in machinery, and workmen opposing them, he was not present to say that these had not been opposed by workmen. But it was fair to say that the same had taken place with regard to both sides. In a co-operative concern, however, he would give a premium for the production of anything of the kind. He should say that 26 years ago this idea was in print, and it was circulated through the engineering trade. It was to the effect that in the case of machines being made by a co-operative society, if an improvement upon a machine were discovered by any member, that improvement should be considered by a committee ; and, if it was valuable, the individual should be rewarded. The reward having been given, it should then belong to the society, and, of course, a patent would be taken out in due course. He considered that the plan which he advocated was the best plan, and the sooner they set to work to bridge over the deep gulf to which Mr. Goldschmidt had referred as being between the two classes, the better. (Loud applause.)

Mr. LEOPOLD HAMEL said that he had listened with pleasure to the able arguments which had been brought forward during the discussion, and it must be admitted that great ability had been displayed on both sides. It was but natural that they should have expected, from such an authority as Mr. Ward, a clear and exhaustive statement of facts ; and if their expectations had even been surpassed, he thought it must be admitted that the talent displayed by the representatives of the working men in discussing the question had been fully "worthy of his steel." (Hear, hear.) No doubt Mr. Ward would be well able to hold his own in the reply to be made, but when all this was over there would still remain much to be done. It would be his endeavour, in the few remarks he had to offer, to point out some kind of result to which these discussions might be made to lead. (Hear, hear,) It would be a great pity if these debates, upon which so much thought and talent had been employed, should end in a mere waste of words. (Hear, hear.) He would, therefore, try to make as few observations as possible with respect to the minor topics dealt with, but it would be necessary for him to say something on the question of the relationship of capital and labour. This relationship was of vital importance to all civilised nations, inasmuch as the welfare of the people entirely depended upon the prosperity and extent of their trade, which prosperity might be much reduced, or even annihilated, by the blind action of the two classes which were more particularly interested—employers and employed. There could be no doubt that in this country the large employers, in times past—times, thank God, never to occur again—had much to answer for. In the words of Mr. Ward, they, by their action, were sowing the wind, and now the employers found themselves surprised to have to reap the whirlwind. (Hear, hear.) It was through them that he believed, even in the present century, labour was kept in worse than bondage ; and, as they were reminded by Mr. Hugh Browne, at a late period there was a statute making it penal for men to attempt to raise their wages or to lessen the hours of labour. Men, women, and children were kept in the depths of mines to work, not like human beings, but like beasts of burden ; and when they came to receive their wages they were met by what was called the " truck system," until at last the working men, in self-defence, were driven into combinations against the masters. No sooner had this been done—no sooner had working men found out the power which they acquired by this means, than the oppressed, as would generally happen in such a case, became the aggressor, and thus a warrant warfare had been carried on between the two classes, sometimes one and sometimes the other being victorious, but the result was always a heavy loss to both sides. (Applause.) Moreover, a feeling was promoted of class against class which, if not checked in time, would go far to drive the trade of this country to foreign climes. (Hear, hear.) He had had occasion to comment, very briefly, on the ability with which arguments had been adduced by both sides, and he was proud to be able to say that those arguments were adduced in a temperate manner, which would do honour to any assembly. (Hear, hear.) Yet it struck him that the various champions had been acting too much as advocates pleading the causes of their clients. (Hear, hear.) Mr. Ward, with all his fairness, had placed the faults and aggressions of unionists in too strong a light, and the faults of the employers slightly in the shade.

On the other hand, the workman had dwelt too much on his own grievances and hardships, while he had swiftly, though gracefully, slided over those of the employers. (Laughter, and hear, hear.) Another thing had struck him—that those who argued on the same side were often at utter variance when it came to particulars. One workman would oppose piecework as having a very bad effect, while another would consider it his best protection. He could not himself enter upon these particulars, not having sufficient practical experience to talk of them, but the facts which he had noticed certainly showed to him that it was difficult to draw a hard and fast line in the matter—that each branch of industry had its own peculiarities, and that often, in individual instances, cases would turn up which must be met on their own merits, by a mutual and honourable understanding. (Hear, hear.) Was this, he asked, a matter of impossibility? He thought not. He had found, with great pleasure, that both classes had a laudable and general desire to do justice to each other, and that both seemed equally to deprecate all violent measures. Mr. Hemm, for instance, would, if possible, do away with all strikes, and he was sure that the employers would equally wish to do away with all lock-outs. (Hear, hear.) Now, here seemed the basis of a common starting point, and judging from what Mr. Hemm had said that night, a useful lesson might be learnt by contemplating the vast amounts which had been expended in the warfare carried on between employer and employed. The cost of one strike was stated to have been no less a sum than £52,000, the benefit of which was lost to the men, while some of them in that strike had to live on 5s. a week. When he came to think to what useful purposes, for the amelioration of the condition of the working people themselves, these vast amounts could be turned, it seemed to him that there must be a bridge such as had been alluded to by Mr. Hemm—that there must be some means of enabling the two parties to come to some general and common understanding. (Hear, hear.) Co-operation would do much, but it would never entirely supersede private enterprise—and, in fact, co-operation simply stepped into the place of the capitalist. He agreed with Adam Smith that the property a man had in his own labour, being the foundation of all other property, was the most sacred. The patrimony of the working man was in the strength and dexterity of his hands, and to hinder him from

exercising that strength and dexterity to the best advantage and as he
choose, would be a violation of his sacred rights ; while, on the other
hand, it would be a violation of the equally sacred rights of the capitalist
to interfere in any way with the use that he made of his wealth, or to
limit his profits. Mr. Mather would excuse him if he pointed out to
him that this was the weak portion of his otherwise so very able arguments, that the workman should do without the capitalist, that he should
take the production of his labour direct to the consumer. He might as
well desire to do away with money altogether as a circulating medium,
and go back to the mode of giving so much grain for a sheep, or so
much wool for his clothing. For it was the capitalist who collected the
surplus production of one market to send it to such where it may be
most required. It seemed, therefore, that it would be very much like
quarrelling with their own bread, to attempt to do away with the very
medium that found them a ready market for their productions and
labour. Nay, he would go much further than that, and would point out
to those who so strenuously are opposed to all wealth in the abstract, to
consider well whether it would not be a wise policy to attract, and to
encourage by all possible means, and by stimulation of very large profits,
the wealthy capitalist to invest his wealth for the purpose of carrying
the productions of England over the whole inhabitable globe. No one
could deny that it was by the aid, and through the instrumentality of
the wealthy capitalist, that the highways of England had been traversed
by railways, giving employment to so many thousands of persons. The
ocean, by their enterprise, was ploughed by steam fleets ; and he would
ask whether Manchester, without their wealth, would be what it is ?
After all, it was but natural that the employer and employed should
have only one interest—their interests were identical. Not that the employer would not naturally try to get the labour he required done in the
cheapest possible manner ; and the labourer had an equal right to get
the best value he could for his work, just as a merchant would get the
best price he was able for his goods, and just as the consumer would
obtain the goods which he required at the cheapest possible rate. Yet
it would be a wise policy for the merchant to ask only a fair and reasonable price for his goods, and for the consumer to pay a good price for
that which was worth it. So, also, it would be a wise policy for em-

ployer and employed to deal justly with each other. (Hear, hear.) He had already occupied enough of the time of his hearers, and he would shortly conclude, not staying to dwell upon the subject of the unequal distribution of wealth, as to do anything of the kind would only lead him away from the object which he had in view. Still, as to this they might take it for granted that the present distribution of wealth was wisely ordained, in spite of the very subtle arguments of Mr. Smith. So long as the world existed, and so long as one man possessed more gifts and greater ability than another, or was more favoured by fortune, so long would some continue to become more wealthy and powerful than others. (Hear, hear.) He would suggest whether, in the existing conditions of society, they might not try to remedy, to some extent, the evils which seemed at present to be connected with combinations. These could not be done away with, nor, indeed, would it be desirable to do so. Mr. Hemm had given a detailed explanation of the working of trades' unions, and the objects contemplated and effected thereby. They could not do away with trades' unions, which were a necessity ; nor did he think that legislation would help them, for, with all respect for the wisdom of our legislators, he would submit to Mr. Ward's sagacity, that you cannot legislate amity between masters and men, and he agreed with the remarks of Mr. Start that all laws which were framed for, or aimed at, any particular body of people must of necessity be one-sided, and as such would only lead to an ill-feeling between the two classes. Now this was, above all others, the one thing to be avoided. He would, therefore, suggest that men who possessed the confidence of both sides, like Mr. Ward and Mr. Hemm—he would not name others in that room who had the honour, integrity, and talent to make themselves useful in this matter—but let such men as Mr. Ward and Mr. Hemm meet face to face and form a real union—a union between employers and employed, to watch over the general welfare, and to calmly and temperately discuss questions affecting the interests of both classes. (Applause.) And if danger threatened any particular branch, let them, shoulder to shoulder, front the foe or invite the friend. (Applause.) If the initiative which had been taken, and so nobly carried out by the Literary Section of that Club, should lead to some such result, then, indeed, Mr. Ward's admirable paper, and the great ability displayed during the discussion,

would not have been in vain. (Applause.) True, he might be met by
the cry of visionary. But he thought the country was ripe for calm discussion and for the consideration of his suggestion. Already the evil
effects of the excessive high prices for the means of production were felt
all over the country, and they could hardly at present fathom the evil
effects of the reaction. Not that high prices in themselves were an evil,
but when they were stimulated to excess they were sure to be followed
by an evil effect, which might last for a long period after. Look at the
trade reports of the present year as compared with those of 1873 and
1872. The total export trade of this country for the first four months
of the present year were £76,000,000 as compared with £84,000,000 in
1873, and £78,000,000 in 1872 ; and if they came to consider the progress which a country like this should make in the natural way, the
falling off would amount to the fearful sum of £16,000,000 for the four
months, or say, in round figures, of £50,000,000 for the whole year—a
seventh of the whole of the export trade of this country. Now, what
was the cause of this ? He affirmed, simply the excessive high prices.
which were felt over the whole civilised world, and now carried with
them the reaction. Now, if ever, was the time for a combined action.
He had been encouraged in making his proposition by the feeling displayed in that room, and should now only venture to say to the employer
that unless he himself reached to the workman a conciliatory, helping
hand, he would become more aggressive with every year ; and to the
working man he would point out the necessity of the capitalist earning
a profitable remuneration, without let or hindrance, for lending the
sinews which carried British productions over the whole of the inhabitable globe, and that by annoying him, he would only kill the sap of the
tree which gave him shade. If they could keep those principles steadily
in view, and if the workman of to-day would but see that by these
peaceable means he might become the proud master of to-morrow, he
would be the first to throw down the barrier which divided class from
class, as mentioned by Mr. Goldschmidt, and would take good care that
it should never be raised again. (Loud applause.)

Mr. COUNCILLOR PARKER said that he had read Mr. Ward's
paper very carefully, and though for the most part he could not but

agree with the opinions there set forth, he was somewhat disappointed because they were not more closely reasoned out. To his mind, in order to carry conviction, the paper should have been more argumentative. It seemed to him rather a declaration of opinions, than an attempt to prove them correct. This would be perhaps quite sufficient, if the discourse were directed alone to people holding similar views, but as it was intended more especially for those of quite a contrary social creed, who would require much convincing, more pains should have been taken in this respect. There would, however, be ample opportunity to repair this deficiency in the reply. Mr. Ward had told them that profits on money capital are lower in England than elsewhere. This, he thought, must be true, for a country banker would lend twenty shillings for a whole week, and would get for the outlay of his money and the liability of losing it the enormous sum of one farthing ; and if the money were paid over in half the time, he would only have half the farthing to receive for the use of it. (Laughter.) The niggliest of the niggardly would hardly think this too much. (Renewed laughter.) Yet the banker, although he had a good knowledge of business in general, and was armed with the needful capital to invade any business he might take a fancy to, preferrred rather to leave the risk and anxiety of general trade, and remained content to take the more simple course of lending his money to others on those easy conditions. The banker was as fond of money as other men, and would not be content with those conditions if not well aware that, in the long run, his mode of trading would be as profitable as any other. It was possible for a man to go into business with but little capital, and in time make a large fortune upon very small profits. Suppose an energetic, clever young man started at twenty-one and continued in business till seventy-one, when he found himself the possessor two hundred thousand pounds. If during this time he had employed, on an average, a thousand workmen, he need but make weekly out of each 1s. 6½d. to give him the whole sum ; but if, at the start, he had been induced by some deputation to give each hand 1s. 6½d. a week more wages, without charging more for his goods, he would not only in the end have had nothing, but would have been several hundred pounds short of what must have been due to his creditors—(laughter)—to say nothing of being unable to lay anything by on the road as a means of sustaining him through the various commercial storms and tempests that must arise in the experience of every tradesman—a circumstance which would alone be sufficient to sink him many times over in the course of his voyage. This was the picture of a successful man, whose descendants, if industrious men of business, might become millionaires. But for one of this kind he would find a hundred who drag out a struggling existence and saved nothing, or who sink by the way and become quite forgotten. (Hear, hear.) There were, no doubt, some fancy trades where large profits were got out of the work of each hand; but those were trades of a precarious nature, where profits, though large, were irregular and sometimes wholly suspended. They were not always unattended with actual weekly loss, besides being in some degree liable to having costly machinery superseded and made of no more worth than old metal. (Hear, hear.) But in those trades large wages were paid, so that the men could easily become independent of their employers, if they thought that they did not get their fair share of the proceeds. By a little forethought and self-denial they could become their own employers, and thus get the high wages and large profits all to themselves. None would see the force of this so clearly as those who thought that business was but an affair of routine, that might be carried on by any one who could once get into the groove. Much was heard of the lacemakers, many of them getting from £3 to £5 a week. Take them at £3. Single men in earnest to emancipate themselves could, without starving, live upon one-third of their wages, and thus be able to lay by the means of making themselves independent of another for employment as a workman. If they were married, it would be no hardship to subsist upon two-thirds of their income and save one-third, which in time would enable them, either alone or in co-operation, to become their own employers, and by this means pocket both wages and profits. (Hear, hear.) The method of salvation was in their own hands, if they would but adopt the means; it was, therefore, a waste of sympathy to dwell further upon them. Mr. Ward treated the subject of money wages in a rather rough and ready way. He could not imagine that Mr. Ward had taken much trouble to look far into this matter. He (Mr. Ward) said that "Two Australian farmers might exchange corn and cattle on an agreement that for each head of cattle or sack of corn an agreed number of marks should be made on a stone or notches cut in a tree, and they might keep their accounts straight. If one wanted to increase the number of marks he should put down for a given article, the other would probably do the same, and what difference would it make? None. Money is precisely the same thing as the marks, but adapted to more complicated transactions." Here he thought Mr. Ward had been rather remiss. Money was made of gold, and is very different from marks, which, like paper money, could be multiplied to any extent. (Laughter.) Gold was very scarce in comparison with other metals; it required a great deal of labour to discover and get it. It was for this reason that it could be made a safe standard of value, but, like all other commodities, it would be of less value in proportion as it increased in quantity. The gold discoveries that had been made during the last twenty years had caused this metal to be far more plentiful, and necessarily of less value. It was, therefore, needful that more of it should be given in the shape wages, if only to keep the workers in all other branches of business from being the slaves of the gold getter. It would have been as unwise as it would have been impossible to have continued them the same as before. The possibility of high money wages gave, however, another advantage—it had virtually lessened the interest of the National Debt to nearly one-half. Early in the present century, when the debt was at its highest, money was nearly of twice its present value; so that, in fact, the presence of plenty of gold was an indirect saving to the taxpayer of nearly fourteen millions every year; and if the same thing continued for twenty-five years longer, it would make things very pleasant for the taxpayer, but rather troublesome for fund holders, and all people with fixed incomes. This was one of the inevitable changes consequent upon altered circumstances, and not by any means the work of trades' unions. The high money wages would have come all the same without them, but in a more harmonious and equitable manner. (Hear, hear.) Some would have got less than they do now and some would have got more, amongst whom would have, no doubt, figured the poor agricultural labourer. (Hear, hear.) It struck him that if ever we should go to excess in the payment of high money wages, the pressure it would cause upon the great bulk of gold which constitutes the general stock would enable the money lenders of every kind to get a higher standard of interest. Until there were signs of this, he thought they might be assured that they were not too extravagant in the use of money. It had been declared during this discussion that the laws were all framed in favour of capital, and in opposition to the interests of labour. This was a fashionable declaration, but not a true one. The laws concerning labour were made for its express protection. When a man had earned his wages the law said that he should have them, and no excuse, short of a declaration that he had not done the work, was of any avail even to delay the payment for one moment. It was in vain to plead a set-off in the shape of a long standing debt. The workman might owe to his employer a large sum of money for goods supplied, but this did not hinder him from being legally entitled to his wages, and it formed no acceptable excuse on the part of the employer for non-payment. If the employer of a number of hands became bankrupt at a time when he owed a large sum to his workmen for wages, though every creditor's account were ever so much over due, the workmen could demand their wages in full, if to pay this there should not be a penny left for any one else. The law said in very plain terms that the workman must be first paid, leaving the capitalist to shift for himself as best he could. In cases of bankruptcy, not only must he be content with the scraps, but he must wait till they could be collected, and riddled, and take what happened to fall to his share after this process had been completed. It would be better if gentlemen would consider these things before they committed themselves to such opinions; neither would it be out of place to ask, while these laws were in force in favour of labour, whether it was consistent, reasonable, or just for workmen to claim the right of participating in the profits? What responsibilities did they take? None whatever. (Hear, hear.) They claimed to make the best terms possible for themselves, without the slightest regard for the welfare of the employers. Whether the employers made profits or not, was not their concern. If an employer failed because he could not make both ends meet, they never blamed themselves because they took from him higher wages than his selling prices would yield. They would say that that was his concern, not theirs, and that others were paying the same. That was all quite right while they kept their place as workmen, pure and simple; but if they were to go shares of the profits, and take the benefits of capital, let them, in all consistency, take its anxieties and liabilities.

(Hear, hear.) If they were determined to wear the crown, let them be content to first bear the cross—(laughter)—by giving up every law which accorded to wages the preference over all other debts, and be content, in case of failure, to keep a fund on hand to make up their share of the deficiency. (Applause.) Limitation of apprentices had found its advocates in this discussion. He was surprised that a system so detrimental to the general good should have had any support. It would in all fairness be admitted that, if it was right to limit in a few trades, it was equally so in all, in order to prevent them from being overrun by the surplus numbers denied admittance in the protected trades. If this regulation became general, what must become of the outcasts who, through these restrictions, were not allowed to learn a trade at all? Were they to become beggars, paupers, or thieves? (Hear, hear.) One of these degrading conditions must be the lot of these unlucky outsiders. If they became beggars or paupers, we ought in justice to support them, asking no questions for conscience' sake. (Laughter.) Or, if the more combative natures took to stealing, society could give them but a feeble rebuke, when it took into consideration that its own favourite institutions had deprived them of the only means by which an honest living could be got. (Hear, hear.) The system, thoroughly carried out, would place on hand a large staff of idlers, who would have to be supported, and well looked after, out of a diminished general stock, made smaller by the forced inactivity of those for whom it was supposed there was no room. Labour, they were constantly being told, was the source of all wealth. That being the case, it seemed strange that men should take means to hinder each other from producing it in the vain hope of getting more for each by diminishing the quantity to be distributed amongst the whole. (Hear, hear.) It was a kind of logic he was unable to understand. It was time men ceased to be frightened out of their wits at shadows. If employers were ever so hungry after apprentice labour, they could only get it to a very limited extent. There were seven years between the age of 14 and 21, while between the ages of 21 and 56 there were five sevens. Men on an average would work till then, so that there must be, in the nature of things, five workmen to one apprentice, to say nothing of the length of time it would take before the apprentice could acquire the needful skill to do efficiently even the

minor parts of the work. (Laughter and applause.) When speed and
skill were considered, it was not fair to suppose that if every youth in
the country were apprenticed at the age of 14, and engaged at work till
21, that more than one-tenth of the work required of the whole country
could be done by such. He should rather think a deal less than much
more, though all the scheming that greediness could suggest was employed to screw it out of them. (Laughter.) A great deal had been
laid at the door of capital during this discussion—more faults than he
could find time either to defend or to deny. There was, however, one
charge in the list to which, in all justice, it must plead guilty. They
were told that capital was mainly answerable for the increase of
pauperism. While he quite agreed with the justice of the charge, he
did not think that there was so much to be alarmed at, or such a deal to
grumble about. It seemed to him strictly in accordance with the nature
of things that pauperism should increase in proportion as wealth accumulated and human sympathies grew. Where there was no wealth
there could be no pauperism, for nobody had anything to spare—
(laughter)—and the would-be pauper must die for the want of those
supplies which would give him this objectionable name. Where there
was no sympathy there could be but little pauperism. The close-fisted
eking out of the commissioned public almoners would be found sufficient
to keep it down. But where sympathy and wealth grew up together,
there would be no grudging of the needful supplies, because a spirit of
liberality and giving would prevail. The ideal standard of comfort
would be raised. That condition which would once have been considered
fair and tolerable would now be regarded as distressing in the extreme,
and a disgrace to the people amongst whom it was allowed to continue.
These sentiments, coupled with more ample means, inspired the public
mind with quicker sympathies for all distress, and prompted a speedier
provision for its relief. We shall always have the poor with us. It
could not be otherwise where human life from its infancy upwards was
so tenderly cared for. There were many newborn infants kept alive
only by the most careful attention and anxious looking after. They had
but a poor stock of vitality to start with, and this requires constantly
nursing to keep it warm—(laughter)—enough to carry it up to maturity.
But in spite of every effort, many of them were too weak to grapple with

the average circumstances of life. Where human life was but of little note, many of these would die off and be forgotten, if indeed they were ever remembered. No tell-tale Press would record the fact and circumstances of their removal. They would be buried without ceremony, and their place of living would be as bare as though they had never been. But the thing with us was altogether different. Our human instincts prompted us to bestow care and attention in proportion to the tenderness of the plants it was our desire and our duty to rear. They were not given up while a shadow of hope remained. These efforts were often so far successful that we see many of them grow up to the enjoyment of a good measure of health and happiness ; but while this was so, not a few drag out but a poor existence. They were below the average in health and strength and intellect. Some thought them idle, some thought them vicious, while the truth of the matter was that they were constitutionally inactive, and only half alive. (Laughter.) In the strife of competition they were unable to produce all they needed to consume, and were more to be pitied than censured. Our old women tell us that wherever there was a Jack there was a Jill. (Laughter.) These Jacks and Jills finally unite, and become the propagators of the like of themselves, and thus perpetuate a race of weaklings, out of whom must needs spring, educate them as they might, a plentiful supply of paupers. (Loud laughter.) This would go on increasing, just in proportion to the amount of sympathy and support a wealthy and generous people were prepared to supply. (Hear, hear.) But, after all, the healthy and strong who had them to support might well be thankful to be able, for it was more blessed to be able to give than to be in need of receiving. (Laughter.) And even the strongest of all, whose never-resting commercial activity prompted them to be foremost in every undertaking, and, so to speak, carry the world on their shoulders, and to whose lot it would fall to pay the largest share to their support, might be thankful, not more for their own strength, than that others were weaker than they; for if, in the order of Providence, all had been their equals in strength and cleverness, and had been prompted by a similar ambition, there would have been no room for them to shine, and this world would have been a very warm spot. (Laughter.) The heat engendered by such never-resting commercial friction would have sent the smoke of their

K

torment ascending ever upwards—(laughter)—and without some pru-
dential means of regulating numbers, population would long ago have
out-grown the means of subsistence, and in spite of never-tiring industry,
universal poverty would have come in like an armed man. (Laughter,
and hear, hear.)   Fortunately, however, it was not so ordained. We
are not all alike.   Our tastes and desires vary as much as our abilities,
and no doubt human happiness was more equally distributed than was
generally supposed.   (Applause.)   The great bulk of mankind were
constitutionally unable to save.   Whether they earned little, or whether
they earned much, they liked to spend it as it came.   They enjoyed life
better this way, while it fell to the lot of the few who could save and
plan to have the anxiety of business, and to take care of the property;
and, like the wise servant whom their Lord had made ruler over all His
house, it became their duty to give every one his meat in due season.
(Loud applause.)

Mr. W. HILL referred, in terms of commendation, to the manner in
which the debate, on both sides, had been conducted.   In noticing one
or two features of unionism, he gave an illustration which had been
brought under his own observation as to the effects of a limitation of
apprentices.   He said that the question of limitation had been touched
upon by various speakers at previous meetings, and he would not
maintain that there ought to be no restriction whatever, though upon
principle he should do so.   In many trades a relaxation of the rules
bearing on the matter would be good, not only for the masters but
also for the men.   He thought that the great evil of trades' unions
was that there should be a hard and fast line drawn, to be applied to all
circumstances, albeit these circumstances might be widely different.
Now, with regard to what Mr. Hemm had said as to one point—that
where men were discharged or otherwise, inquiries were made as to the
cause—he would ask, from whom were those inquiries made ?   He had
personally found that where inquiries were made, it was pretty much of
the men themselves; and, however good might be the case of the
master, it was made a sort of "black" job.   (Laughter.)   As a rule, he
got on very well with his men, though in the course of a number of
years they had had some little disagreements.   But where that had

occurred he was sure that had the committee had communication with him beforehand, it would not have taken place. (Hear, hear.) He would call his own men in as witnesses, but it must be privately, and not before the whole shop, because he should want the men to say what they thought without restraint. He would state that he had been very much pleased to hear the observations of Mr. Hemm; and he did think that now there was a better feeling than had hitherto existed, and that trades' unionists were more disposed to look upon these matters in a reasonable light. (Hear, hear.) He was sure that if, along with this improved condition of things, trades' unionists would but take some pains to get at the employer's reasons and motives for a certain line of action which he might adopt, they would generally be found to agree. (Applause.)

Mr. WHITTINGHAM said he should like the Chairman to express some opinion as to whether it was intended to carry on this discussion throughout the summer, or to an interminable extent? It was a question that could not be exhausted, and, moreover, it was one of much interest, as manifested by the present meeting—especially considering that the question had been so frequently discussed there before. He should like an answer on the point he had raised, for several members of the club interested in these meetings for discussion, and in their success, considered that it was desirable to have a diversity of subjects. He was aware that some time back several gentlemen expressed a wish to read papers on different subjects. If at some future date they recurred to the subject he thought it would be advantageous, but he did not know whether it was intended that Mr. Ward should reply to all that had been said. It seemed to him that the debate had better be deferred, either that night or after the next meeting, until Autumn.

The CHAIRMAN, in reply, said that the Committee desired to fix no limit to the discussion, so long as it proved interesting, and attracted such large numbers. It was their wish that, so far as was practicable, every gentleman should have an opportunity of expressing his opinions on the subject, and also as to Mr. Ward's paper. (Applause.) That promise had been given. Supposing the discussion terminated that night, or next Tuesday, or the Tuesday afterwards, what Mr. Whittingham wanted could not take place, for the Committee did not contemplate having more discussions until the Autumn. The following session would be opened at a convenient season, when, no doubt, there would be that diversity which was suggested. Now, however, he thought that they should endeavour to exhaust the subject introduced by Mr. Ward, instead of occupying a large portion of next session with it. (Hear, hear.)

Mr. JOHN RENALS said, as to the termination of the debate, he was not surprised that lawyers should desire to close it, for if they went on like this he should begin to expect that they would not want much litigation. (Laughter.)

SEVENTH NIGHT'S DISCUSSION.

(TUESDAY, JUNE 2, 1874.)

MR. W. WHITEHEAD, CHAIRMAN, said that some gentlemen appeared to be of opinion that it would be for him, at the
close, to sum up; but he thought if he were to summarise the debate,
he should be usurping the position of Mr. Ward, whereas, his only
duty was to act as umpire, keeping the balance even on all sides.
(Applause.)

Mr. H. T. YATES then said that he should not like to detain his
hearers long, but there were a few topics upon which he had thought
that he should like to say a word or two. He must say that, in his
opinion, one of the most important matters was not simply the subject
matter of discussion, but the very fact of the discussion itself; and he
looked upon it as a great and valuable acquisition that gentlemen representing both labour and capital should have met there in such a manner,
to discuss the subject as temperately as it had been discussed hitherto.
(Hear, hear.) He must notice the ability which had been so remarkably
shown, particularly from the workmen's side. For himself, he was not
prepared at the outset to listen to the able and temperate arguments
which had been advanced, and at the same time to hear so much of
common sense as had characterised many of the speakers on their side.
In thinking over this subject, it had struck him that it would not be
amiss, while regarding the question in its present aspect, to look back a
little upon the past, and see how the matter then stood as to combinatons
of labour. He believed it was some sixty years ago that we first knew,
locally, about combinations of labour. He found that Nottingham and the
neighbourhood were at that time subject to an organisation which spoke very
little for the knowledge of the people, or for their good sense in carrying

it forward. But they knew that education was then in a very lamentable state—that the people engaged in, or connected with, this organisation entertained very queer views on the subject of capital and labour. They were organised, as was known, into armed bands, and very sad deeds were committed by them. Since then there had been strikes, with violence. Such a condition of things, however, having passed away, and a considerable interval having now elapsed since the period referred to, he thought they might well bury some of those dead subjects, which had been reaped up, perhaps, more than was necessary. He would ask them to look at the more recent struggle of the agricultural labourer. Mistakes had in the past been made, no doubt, on the side of labour, and also on the side of capital. Nevertheless, looking at the question of the agricultural labourer, they had seen of late a dispute in which, so far as they knew, there had been no intimidation, and surely the circumstance was suggestive. It showed, to his mind, that the question of capital and labour was better understood now than formerly; and though things had taken place such as those to which he had referred, they were assembled now to discuss the subject calmly together. (Hear, hear.) He was of opinion that they would reap a very great advantage from this discussion of the question. For himself, he had no idea of taking part in the debate, but becoming interested, he also became desirous of adding what little he could, as others had done before him—in other words, he became desirous of stating any views which he might entertain. He was strongly inclined to think that the more they could bring public opinion to bear on the matter, the more likely were they to have temperate action on the part of both employers and employed. (Hear, hear.) Public opinion was now, he thought, so far advanced that strikes in great districts could not take place in the present day against, and in face of, public opinion. (Hear, hear.) At least, he did not think they would be successful unless public opinion were to determine in their favour. They had had some heavy charges made against capital. It had been urged that capital made too large a profit, and some very fanciful pictures had been drawn, from which it would almost seem that many people believed it only necessary to go into business for wealth to tumble in. (Hear, hear, and laughter.) But he thought that by investigation it would be found, as a rule, that large profits did not mean large fortunes ; and that the largest fortunes were generally made where profits were small. All this might, and no doubt would, seem a paradox, but so he believed it was. The more they approached to raw material, and the less there was of labour, the more manufacturers came out with wealth. They might, for the sake of example, take the case of our own town. In the Nottingham lace trade there was an immense amount of capital invested, and the lace machines employed were of such beautiful construction that they almost seemed like sensitive beings ; yet they could not but be surprised, in considering the large amount of capital invested, when they looked back upon the past and found how few were the men who had got out of the trade with whole skins, and with fortunes at the back of them. He thought it an erroneous idea, on the part of several speakers, that large profits as a rule meant large fortunes ; on the contrary, he maintained that large fortunes were mainly the result of a man's frugality or saving habits, and were the accumulation of a long period of time, rather than the result of a high rate of profit derived from a particular trade. (Hear, hear.) Speaking of combinations, Mr. Ward said that so far as trades' unions had for their objects the raising of the working classes in the social scale, and to resist on their behalf oppression and injustice, they had his sympathy ; and he (Mr. Yates) thought so far as they had these for their objects, they had the sympathy of every employer. As to the sacredness of a man's property in his own mental and bodily powers, he thought all employers must recognise this principle. It was only when the principle was overstepped, and when there was an interference which prejudiced the rights of others, that any objection could reasonably be taken to trades' unions. If they conceded to unionists the right which they had of fixing the average price of their labour, and also the right to strike where, in a dispute, other means had failed, these combinations might still be unjust to particular trades, and to the prejudice of the interests of society at large. The reason he had in saying this was, that he believed trades' unions had no power to settle the price at which a particular article or commodity could be paid for. (Hear, hear.) It was settled by powers other than those of either capitalists or workers. There was the question of the law of supply and demand to be taken into consideration. Mr. Ward said in one part of his paper, that theoretical political economists affirmed that the law of supply and demand redressed all grievances in this matter. Without professing to know much about political economy, it struck him that the operation of this law of supply and demand did really settle the value or price of an article. (Hear, hear.) If there was in the market a very large supply of a particular kind of labour, the consequence inevitably was, that the price of that description of labour had to come down. This held good also with respect to merchandise and other commodities. If a manufacturer or a merchant had a quantity of goods in stock of which he was very anxious to dispose, he forced them into the market, and the result was that prices receded. If this was so, it placed them face to face with an important question, which was, What power have unions, if any, to regulate prices? He observed that a Mr. Moult, Secretary to the Birmingham Builders' Society, stated in evidence before the Trades' Union Commissioners, that ten per cent. of the building trade in the country were in the union; and he gave a list of the wages paid in different localities, which varied, for the same class of work, from $4\frac{1}{2}$d. to 8d. per hour. Now if trades' unions could not affect values, or only partially, and if they could not settle values, they could only equalise the wages to be paid to the men generally—or, rather, locally. (Applause.) If unionists acted fairly in this matter, they would not fix the average wages at the lowest man, but would take an average between the best and the worst. If they took the average in any other way, he held that it was unjust. (Hear, hear.) This was one of the objections which he took to trades' unions. They had heard from Mr. Woodhead, however, that there were unions where uniformity of price for labour was not recognised, and he was glad to find that this was the case. A clever man, with whom he had spoken once, told him that he did not belong to the union in his branch of trade, because he considered himself better than most of the workmen in that body, and could get more money without being a member. He affirmed that the principle upon which the average rate of wages was based was not the best principle for the workman. It did not tend to develop in him those qualities of forethought and industry, and those other qualities a man had developed in him by the knowledge that he was going to do the best he could for himself. (Hear, hear.) If there was anything which made men strive, it was the knowledge that they would have for themselves and their families what they strove for. (Applause.) He did not know of anything that was more sacred in this matter than a man's work, whether the man were an employer or a workman. If that a man worked was the reason of his belonging to the working classes, he thought that he himself, though an employer, might claim to be a labourer. But what he wished to see, and what he thought they all wished to see, nationally, was that the restrictions against ability should be removed. (Hear, hear.) As to a recent alteration in our army system, they had seen that it was not simply the question of purchase which had wrought that alteration, but that one of the causes had been the general desire that the best man should get to the top of the tree. (Hear, hear.) He approved of the principle, and that what a man could do he should be rewarded for. The objection he had taken ran through the whole question of piecework. Here he contended that a man who had work to do was bound, at least morally, to do it in the best and most expeditious manner. They had heard it said that the reason the men objected to the system of piecework was that employers, when they got a man to exert himself as much as he could, dropped the wages paid—or, rather, the rate of wages. Mr. Hemm had somewhat qualified his remarks on this head, saying that to do so was not general. But he would ask the representatives of workmen, and also the employers present, whether they had never seen the effect of the magic touch of piecework? As to the objections made against the system, if there were unjust employers, there were also unjust workmen, and the question of piecework could only be met by fair and honourable conduct on both sides. (Applause.) One of their friends had said that the men did not care for the quality or material of their work under the system, so long as that work served until they were paid. Now his experience had taught him that if a man in one position was dishonest and dishonourable, he would be the same in another. (Hear, hear.) He knew it was impossible that in many cases piecework should altogether be the custom of trades, but where it could be settled by weight, measure, or quantity, he maintained that it was fairest for both masters and men. Under the system an employer was better enabled to ascertain what would be the cost of an article. (Hear, hear.) It seemed to be alleged that the workmen did not get sufficient remuneration for their labour, or an adequate share in the division of profit. There was

one remark made by an able speaker, Mr. Connelly, who had said that
what the masters want is more profit, and what the men want is more
wages. (Laughter and applause.) It was very true, and the question
to be solved was, how was this matter to be met? If a man having a
certain article to sell could reduce the price of it, that price went to the
public eventually, but a man's great duty was to do the best he could for
himself, be he man or master. (Hear, hear.) Supposing the conditions
imposed were obstacles in the way of doing what he had to do in the
best and most expeditious manner, then the sooner those obstacles were
removed the better. Though advantage might be taken at times by
masters who were hard or unjust to their workmen, at the same time he
believed that if a proper spirit existed, this system of piecework would
be a great advantage to workmen themselves, and in a certain measure
they would also participate in the benefits of a trade. (Hear, hear.)
Looking at the whole question broadly, they knew that in England it
was much more difficult to live upon low wages than was the case
abroad. They knew that in this country necessity compelled men to
ask high wages, as it compelled masters to give them, and the only
advantage we have was owing to machinery and certain natural productions. But England was pressed hardly on the continent, and some
of his hearers would know of businesses that had been removed from this
country on account of the cheaper labour. Not that he did not think
the dearer labour of England had a certain advantage, nevertheless. It
was not merely a question of the price paid for labour, it was the work
and the quality of it. (Hear, hear.) In reading a book by a celebrated
railway contractor, Mr. Brassey, he was struck by the fact that the whole
book seemed to settle the point that there was a general average price
for labour. In France he once met with a gentleman who had sub-
contracted under Mr. Brassey, and who had told him pretty much the
same thing. This gentleman had said to him that he had not always
found it best to pay Frenchmen, at the same work, only half the rate of
wages paid to Englishmen. A skilled English navvy would of course be
better than a Frenchman who was unaccustomed to the work; but it
was not simply a question of ability, as the Frenchman could not undergo
nearly so much physical fatigue as the English labourer. In making
this observation he did not wish to be offensive at all to any one. In

face of the cheaper labour on the continent, so far as raw material was concerned, we in England were excellently situated. He would not longer detain his hearers, but he would be glad if, as a result of this discussion, they found that their efforts had at all, or in any degree, had a desirable effect with regard to the question of capital and labour. (Applause.)

Mr. WILLIAM CLARKE, as a representative workman, said he must remark, in the first place, that he had very much enjoyed the present discussion, through the kindness of the Honorary Secretary of the Literary Section of that Club, Mr. E. Killingley. He had been gratified at the manner in which the discussion had gone forward, but there were one or two things which had been touched upon as to which he should like to have a word or two, and one was the average or minimum rate of wages question. He very much agreed with his friend Mr. Woodhead on this subject, but though a little had been put forward in its support on the part of trades' unions, he did not think it could be thoroughly defended. He had paid close attention to a few matters with respect to unions and the relationship between capital and labour, and in very many instances in the past the minimum rate of wages had been too much the rule with the majority of masters or employers. He had seen establishments where men were at work, some better at their trade than others, and men who were inactive and indolent had obtained the same wages, frequently, as those who where their superiors. It was, however, somewhat to be expected on the side of trades' unions that they should adopt the minimum rate of wages system, for if they did not, he was sure there were employers that would do it. But he did not complain so much as some of its adoption. There was another matter which had been discussed, that of piecework. As to this he thought that something could be said. A case had come to his knowledge, only a few days ago, in which a farmer living some miles away let out a certain portion of work, to a very active and useful labourer. This man exerted himself to the utmost, and, being skilful, he made 4s. per day. Finding that he had done this, the master thought it was too much for the labourer to make, so he got rid of him and put another man on the same class of work, paying him 2s. 9d. per day. This man did scarcely half the work of the other who had been discharged, when the master complained, saying that so-and-so had done so much work in the day. But the man replied, " Surely you don't expect me to do as much work for 2s. 9d. per day as the other did for 4s., with great exertion." (Laughter and applause.) Now he was afraid that this was the principle too much at work with regard to the system. (Hear, hear.) He thought that the same kind of treatment, or similar would be served out in too many instances providing the unions were to sanction piecework. Stuart Mill laid it down that there was a certain amount of work to be done during the year, for which there was a certain amount of money to be spent ; and that there were a certain number of individuals to do that work, who could do it by mechanical means at their disposal by so many hours a day. Take it that these individuals could manage to do the work by eight or ten hours a day's labour, if they came to have one-third of these men working at the rate of sixteen hours per day, there would necessarily be a good many others who were out of employment altogether. (Hear, hear.) That was the view which he held of piecework, and he thought that it was the view which unions had of it, generally. He had seen men toiling for fifteen or sixteen hours a day in a certain branch of industry, while at the same time there were others of the same trade walking the streets in want of work and of food to eat—men who had served their apprenticeship to the trade, and who had properly and faithfully served their term of seven years. (Hear, hear.) Yet though these men were walking the streets in want of work, others in the same business were actually working as many as fifteen or sixteen hours per day. It could not be wondered at, with instances like those before them, that unionists should take up the matter in the way they did, and protest in such a manner against an undue amount of piecework. (Applause.)

Mr. J. W. JEVONS said he had not attended on the present occasion with the intention of speaking, but rather for the purpose of listening. He observed that this discussion had in its philosophical bearing a most important question for all classes of society. They had been talking about the rates of wages and about trades' unions—which in the matter of wages were mere agencies—but they seemed to forget the fact that at the present time, in this country, we were going through a transition period—a transition period of a momentous character. (Hear, hear.) Up to now it had never been understood what the real rate of wages should be, as compared with the profit of capital. So far as his recollection of history went, he might say distinctly that hitherto rates of wages had been, as a rule, fixed by the employers ; but, with the growth of intelligence on the part of the labouring classes, they had come to know that now they had not only such a share in the division of profits arising from the combined operations of capital and labour as had heretofore been awarded them, but a further share which they were entitled to demand. He did not say that the working classes, or the producing classes, whichever they might be termed, should take any undue advantage of that knowledge, for if they did it would simply recoil upon themselves by driving the trade of this country to other nations. (Hear, hear.) Up to this time, however, there had been no satisfactory settlement of what was the fair proportion of the wage of the labour to the capital profit. For himself, he had looked upon these discussions with much interest, as throwing great light on the subject. A great deal was to be learnt from the speeches which had been delivered, and he thought that the club, in opening its doors for the discussion, and in undertaking the publication of the results, had conferred a great public benefit. (Applause.) He trusted that this series of discussions, which were at length coming to a close, might be continued or reproduced in another form at a future time ; because those gentlemen who had taken the trouble to collect their ideas on the subject knew, however large the audience might be at that place, there was a much larger audience beyond the room. (Hear, hear.) They were assembled in what might be called their Parliamentary session ; and he thought it was desirable that under the term " Capital and Labour," or under any other term, discussions like these should be continued in the next season, after the Summer was over. (Hear, hear.) He had followed the discussions with much interest, and he was sure that they were of the greatest possible value. (Applause.)

Mr. THOMAS HILL said he had listened to the debates from the commencement, but he had not heard it explained in what mode, different from the one at present existing, labour could get more than it did. To him it appeared, from all that he had heard, that labour and capital got exactly what they could, respectively. (Hear, hear.) There was abundance of labour and abundance of capital in this country which never could be regulated by trades' unions. But he still thought that the law of supply and demand regulated prices all the world over. Some people had an idea that one portion of the community obtained an undue amount of remuneration. In early life he lived for some years in Devonshire, where, if he had then been an employer of labour, and had offered 9s. a week, he could have had a whole parish, and should have been thought a generous man. At that time the wages paid were pretty much about 8s. He should judge that now these Devonshire labourers were very likely receiving for their labour 10s. or 12s., and this without the aid of any union at all. At that period smiths were engaged in a certain factory, and a very good smith could be employed at 16s. per week ; but at present 24s. were being paid. There were no unions, and he learnt that the cause of the rise had been that the men could go across the British Channel and get 26s. or 28s. per week. By means of railways, servants could be got from any part of England, whereas people were formerly kept to their own parishes and could not move. (Hear, hear.) Now, however, for 10s. a man could remove himself and his labour fifty miles away. The results he had noticed were owing to the operation of the law of supply and demand working in an unseen way. (Hear, hear.) In Devonshire the farms were chiefly small, ranging from 50 to 150 acres ; and he thought that 100 acres would average the whole county. He knew farmers there who worked harder and fared worse than mechanics in Nottingham. He knew, also, that the land they were cultivating was let to them at 20s. or 30s. an acre, and that the labourer was almost on the point of starvation. What, he asked, was wanted ? It was a thing that had been spoken against— capital. (Hear, hear.) If there had been more capital at work, effecting improvements, the labourer would have got more wages, the farmer more profit, and the land ultimately would be more valuable to the kingdom. (Hear, hear.) The late Mr. John Heathcoat, of Tiverton, purchased a number of farms in the neighbourhood of that place, and they were in a low state. Mr. Heathcoat told the farmers, having bought the property, that if they wanted £100 spending on each of their farms, on showing that it was necessary or required, they could have it at five per cent. The consequence was that his farms were flourishing, and he set an example which was eventually followed by large landed proprietors. (Hear, hear.) The History of the French Revolution would show that at one time, owing to the troubles in the country, and to the fact that the Revolutionary Government issued paper money, the farmers would not send their produce to Paris, because payment was made in paper money, which, as was thought, would be worthless if the Government were overthrown. The Government, which was strong, said to the bakers, "You shall sell a certain sized loaf for a certain price." The baker said he could not afford it, but was told that if he did not do it he would be hanged—(laughter)—and he accordingly used up all his flour. Then the miller shared the same treatment, until at length his supply was gone. The Government next said that they would make the farmers bring their produce to market, and they had to have an army of men to bring food into Paris, the end being that it beat the Revolution. In conclusion, he said that nothing could equalise labour and capital but the operation of the law of supply and demand. (Applause.)

Mr. WILLIAM START said he might venture to pass over the speech of Mr. Yates, as, in replying to some other speakers, he would probably reply, at least in a measure, to some things advanced by Mr. Yates with which he could not agree. Mr. Simons had charged the trades' unions with want of knowledge of the principle of free trade. "Those who live in glass houses should not throw stones." In reply to his (Mr. Start's) statement that he had never known an instance of coercive injustice in connection with the union to which he belonged, Mr. Simons brought forward an instance which he called coercive injustice, in which a union had made a demand of an advance of 2s. per week on the wages of each man. He was compelled to give it, or the men would go out. He asked, "Was not that coercive injustice?" He (Mr. Start) answered, "No." The men had as much right to demand an advance on the price of their labour as any tradesman had to ask an advance on the price of goods. There surely was no violation here of the principle of free trade. Mr. Simons was not compelled to

have the labour if he did not wish to pay the price for it, any more than
a customer was compelled to have any article if the price or quality of it
was not satisfactory. (Hear, hear.) Mr. Simons's instance of coercive
injustice fell to the ground. Mr. Hancock spoke of trades' unions as
seeking to enforce a system of dead-levelling, which led men to trust to a
union rather than to their own abilities. Mr. Hancock surely did not
understand the question at all, or he would not speak of it in the way he
did. (A laugh.) The workmen had already shown that the employers
themselves were responsible for any appearance of dead-levelling, and no
trades' union ever prohibited a man from rising above the common level.
Mr. Hancock argues against that which does not exist. The trades'
unions set only a minimum rate, but never fixed a maximum rate. But
Mr. Hancock said the twisthands fixed the maximum rate. Now twisthands worked piecework. There would scarcely be any fault found with
them, for they worked on the principle that was said to be sound and
most approved. (Hear, hear.) "It had been admitted that men who
worked for, say Jones, were not worth their salt." If Mr. Jones had
got the worst men in the trade, it simply proved that Jones was the
worst master in the trade. (Laughter.) Either Jones was the worst
master in the trade, or Jones had the worst machinery in the trade ; for
the good men would find the good masters and the best machines, and
would work where they got most money. "The laws relating to labour
operate equitably." Not so, for the Masters and Servants Act dealt
partially with offenders. It punished the masters with a fine, and sent
workmen or servants to prison ! They asked for distinctions to be
abolished. (Applause.) In reply to Mr. Gripper, he begged to say
that he was surprised to hear that gentleman make such observations as
were made by him. Mr. Gripper was a gentleman whom he had
watched and admired. He did not reckon to pin his faith to the sleeve
of any man, however, but he had always felt safe when he had walked
upon ground over which Mr. Gripper had trod. On this occasion he
did not feel that gentleman's ground was solid. He failed to see that
hardships inflicted by employers touched the question of the position of
capital as to labour, but saw clearly that hardships inflicted by trade
societies touched the question of the position of labour as to capital.
Mr. Ward's paper was designed to show that injustice on either side did

affect the respective positions of capital and labour. On this point Mr. Gripper was at variance with Mr. Ward. Mr. Gripper said that, " He thought one great omission in his (Mr. Start's) reasoning was that there seemed to be an assumption that there were only the employed and the employers to be considered. The interests of the outside public were apparently ignored." He must say that it was only apparently ignored, and not really so. "If Mr. Start would look carefully through his argument by the light of the knowledge and conviction that there was this third class to consider, probably he would materially modify some of the statements he had brought forward." He begged to say that he had done this, and he found no reason to modify any of his former observations ; perhaps he had not been able to make himself understood. He thought he had not laid it down as a principle that this third class should not be considered, but he had urged that the capitalist was a very improper person to lecture working men on the practice of this virtue. Example was said to be better than precept, and the workmen asked for the example from the other classes. (Hear, hear.) The working man was not in a position to consider this third party, unless there were mutual considerations and concessions. " The subject of the agricultural labourer did not meet the question, for the universal feeling was that they are badly used." But the universal feeling was a mockery until the labourers rose and challenged the oppressor, and sought to stand in the dignity of their manhood. (Applause.) One or two observations from Mr. Hart required a little attention. Mr. Hart thought "that the legislation of the last thirty years had been of a most equitable character." They were happy to say that it had been in the right direction, but had not lost sight of the struggles and agitations that had taken place in order to bring about this better state of things. This better state of things had not been brought about without much sacrifice on the part of the workmen. They remembered the opposition that had been raised against it, and knew the direction of the opposition. They failed to discern the soundness of the reasoning that because, during the last thirty years, some of the injustice against labour had been removed, they should rest and be satisfied. They could never rest until labour was free, could never rest while one oppressive law remained on the statute book, and could never rest until they had perfect equality before

L

the law. They acknowledged that they enjoyed a better state of things
than they once did ; that under legislation they had made some progress,
and enjoyed more freedom in industrial districts. Would that these
liberties were extended to the agricultural labourers, and to all ! Then
would labour take its proper position in the country, and sustain its true
relationship to capital, and would command that respect and remuneration which were its due. (Applause.) They asked only that labour
and capital should work in harmony, and that one should not be the
slave of the other. Mr. Ward's paper had not settled the question of
the rights and responsibilities of capital and labour, and the object of
the paper would be lost, and it would fail to bring capital and labour
into their proper positions, unless some practical work could be done.
The best thing to be done at present seemed to be, to form an association
or a committee to further consider the question, and mutually agree
upon a programme to recommend to the consideration of capitalist and
workman. He had no doubt that the paper was intended to bring
capital and labour closer together, and the paper was as good and
and fair as could be expected from the capitalists' point of view.
Workmen all wanted to acknowledge the principle of free trade,
but free trade would be a curse to the working class if it were not
tempered with humanity. (Applause.) They did not want free trade
with a vengeance, but free trade with consideration and justice.
(Applause.) Let it be understood, once for all, that they had no quarrel
with the principles of Mr. Ward's paper. The principles were as much in
the interest of labour as of capital. The workmen's points of disagree-
ment were simply in the details. (Hear, hear.) They could not allow
unfair aspersions to be cast upon the efforts of labour to defend itself
against the tyranny of capital. He thought that, in the course of this
debate, it had been shown that capital had been guilty of unjustifiable
conduct, and that labour had had to act in self-defence, and for many
years had been fighting against great odds. They acknowledged that, in
the struggle, labour had sometimes made mistakes, but the wonder was
that it had made so few, considering that in many instances it had been
goaded to madness, and had had to struggle for existence. (Applause.)
But labour rose to assert its rights, and to maintain its dignity ; and if
it were not treated with the respect that was due, it must cultivate self-

respect. (Hear. hear.) Mr. Parker's speech was, perhaps, the most debatable of any that had been delivered on these occasions, and if it had been delivered earlier would have received a fair share of criticism. He had said some very wise things, amongst some very foolish things. He had drawn some pictures which were perfectly visionary, and given illustrations which were not analogous to the case in hand. All the facts and statistics that had been produced showed that the improved circumstances of the workers were due in part to the interest taken by the workers in their trades' unions, and in organising the principles of labour. Perhaps one reason why the poor agricultural labourer figured so badly under the altered circumstances was for want of union. In this debate the limitation of apprentices had not been defended as a right, but as an expediency. Something had been said about pauperism being hereditary. He was of opinion that the hereditary argument should not deter the social reformers of this country from making an attempt to destroy the hereditary principle. The fact that paupers were hereditary was no reason that they should not be cared for. They were a dead-weight upon society, and if the leading classes would turn their attention to their elevation, they might be made of some service to the country, society relieved of a great burden, and the people made happier. Mr. Ward said that wages should be as high as the circumstances of the country would allow. There was wisdom in that observation. The wage question cut two ways, for whilst high wages might tend to check production in one direction, it encouraged it in another. Two-thirds of the trade of the country was in luxuries, and if wages were low the working classes could not obtain them. How much could the agricultural labourer encourage trade? It required his 14s. to buy bread. It might be thought that he spoke as one who had a great personal complaint to make, but he had not. He might say that he had always been treated with due consideration by employers, and perhaps always received a fair market price for his labour. He had never had a bad master—well, only one, and he worked for him but four days, and then "sacked" him. He was not bad in the sense that he was unjust, but he was drunken, and it struck him that the place was not safe. It was bad to be forced to work with drunken men, but it was worse to work with drunken masters. A drunken man could sometimes be controlled, but a drunken master could not. From his experi-

ence he should conclude that bad masters were the exception, rather
than the rule ; and he thought those bad masters would grow fewer, as
both masters and men understood their true relationship to each other.
He hoped those discussions would be a means of education to both.
(Applause.)

Mr. S. HANCOCK said that when he was speaking as to the Criminal
Law Amendment Act, Mr. Albert Richards stated that he could show
the statements in reference to it were not correct, and that he could bring
proofs. Inasmuch as the adjournment of the debate was moved by Mr.
Richards, he had time to prove what he affirmed : there could be no
doubt that his remarks as reported might be taken as a fair exposi-
tion of what he said. Now, he (Mr. Hancock) had said that many
Members of Parliament and would-be Members of Parliament had spoken
much that was absurd with respect to the Criminal Law Amendment Act.
(Hear, hear.) The object of his remarks had been to show that, as he
read the Act, it was not a piece of class legislation, specially directed
against unionists, and he failed to see that Mr. Richards's remarks had in
any way affected the question. (Hear, hear.) He contended that the
Criminal Law Amendment Act drew no line as to whether a man was
in a union or not—it did not matter what a man was; the Act dealt
with picketing as an offence. If they took it that picketing was right, it
was altogether another thing ; but he maintained that the system, or
practice was wrong, and the more he looked into it, the more he was
inclined to think such practice unjustifiable. It might have been, however, that, but for the existence of unions, the Act would not have been
passed. Mr. Hugh Browne had borne out that gross outrages had been
committed in districts where unions were not established. Unless picketing and other practices specified in the Act could be defended, the workmen had no cause, in his opinion, to complain. The measure had been
constantly alluded to as a piece of class legislation ; but if he understood
class legislation, it meant that what constituted offence in A was
not offence in B. He was pleased with the suggestion of Mr.
Hamel ; the idea had also been thrown out in one of a series of able
arguments which appeared in *The Engineer* of the 15th ult., on the
subject of strikes. He (Mr. Hancock) said that the " card," as given

out in the lace trade, was the maximum rate paid in any and every shop, and *there*, at least, they did regulate the maximum. (Hear, hear.) He had known instances of coercion. Herbert Spencer said in his work on " Sociology :"—" Feeling keenly what they have to bear, and tracing grievances to men who buy their labour, artizans conclude that those above them, considered individually and in combination, are personally bad, selfish, or tyrannical in special degrees. It never occurs to them that the evils they complain of result from the average human nature of our age. * * * The simple fact, notorious enough, that working men who save money and become masters, are not more considerate than usual towards those they employ, but often the contrary, might alone convince them of this. * * * Enquire about the life in every kitchen where there are several servants, and you will find quarrels about supremacy, tyrannies over juniors who are made to do more than their proper work. * * * The doings in workshops illustrate in various ways the ill-treatment of artizans by one another ; and still more conspicuously is this proved by the internal government of trade combinations. * * * When an association of carpenters or en- gineers makes rules limiting the number of apprentices admitted, with the view of maintaining the rate of wages paid to its members—when it thus tacitly says to every applicant beyond the number allowed, ' Go and apprentice yourself elsewhere'—it is indirectly saying to all other bodies of artizans, ' You may have your wages lowered by increasing your numbers, but we will not.' And when the other bodies of artizans severally do the like, the general result is that the incorporated workers of all orders say to the surplus sons of workers who want to find occu- pations, ' We will *none* of us let our masters employ you.' This carried out could only eventuate in enforced idleness. * * * The class-bias, fostering the belief that the question in each case is entirely between employer and employed, between capital and labour, shuts out the truth that the interests of all *consumers* are involved, and that the immense majority of consumers belong to the working classes. A strike which makes coal dear affects in a relatively small degree the rich consumers, but is keenly felt by the millions of poor consumers, to whom the outlay for coal is a serious item of expenditure. In nearly all products the evil caused by a rise of price falls more heavily on the vast numbers

who work, than on the small numbers who have moderate incomes or
large incomes.' (Much has been said of Communism, of co-operation,
and wages plus a share of the annual profits.) 'Were not their judg-
ments warped by class-bias, working men might be more pervious to the
truth that better forms of industrial organisation would grow up and
extinguish the forms which they regard as oppressive, were such better
forms *practicable;* and they might see that the impracticability of
better forms results from the imperfections of existing human nature,
moral and intellectual.   If the workers in any business could so combine
and govern themselves that the share of profit coming to them as
workers was greater than now, while the interest on the capital employed was less than now, and if they could at the same time sell the
articles produced in business managed as at present, then manifestly
businesses managed as at present would go to the wall.   The success of
industrial organizations higher in type requires in the members a nicer
sense of justice than is at present general.   Closer co-operation implies
greater mutual trust ; and greater mutual trust is not possible without
more respect for one another's claims. * * * While workmen think
themselves justified in combining to sell their labour only on certain
terms, but think masters not justified in combining to buy it only on
certain terms, they show a misconception of equity—the misconception,
namely, that justice requires an equal sharing of benefits among producers, *instead* of requiring, as it does, equal freedom to make the best
of their faculties.   The general policy of trades'-unionism, tending every-
where to restrain the superior from profiting by his superiority lest the
inferior should be disadvantaged, is a policy which, acted out in any
industrial combinations, must make them incapable of competing with
combinations based on the principle that benefit gained shall be proportioned to faculty put forth.   The relation of master and workman
has to be tolerated, because for the time being no other will answer as
well. * * * In any industrial combination there must be a regulating agency.   That regulating agency, whatever its nature, must be
paid for—must involve a reduction from the total proceeds of labour
regulated.   Under better systems there will doubtless be a decrease in
the cost of regulation, but for the present our comparatively costly
system has the justification that it alone succeeds.   With decrease of

defects will come economy of regulation, and consequently greater shares
of profit to themselves." He concluded by disclaiming that he was at
all opposed to workmen forming themselves into unions. It had been
wisely said, "Sweet are the uses of adversity," and he thought that one
of the uses of adversity to working men had been the formation of unions,
but such organisations should be rightly directed. It had been said on
another and very different subject—

> " That marriage, rightly understood,
> Gives to the virtuous and the good,
> A Paradise below."

Now, if their friends the unionists would only rightly understand the
uses of trade unions, it would aid them to realise in like manner something like " a Paradise below." (Laughter and applause.)

Mr. CHATWIN (President of the Amalgamated Society of Joiners)
said that when he spoke previously he was on the subject of piecework,
and treating of the opposition of unions to the system, Mr. Ward ques-
tioned whether this was wise. He had shown, to the best of his ability,
that the workmen considered it was wise, because of the advantage
employers often took when piecework was adopted ; and trades' unions
failed to see any advantage to the workmen in adopting such a system,
to compensate in any way for the amount of trouble that system of
working would cause. As to the average rate of wages, was it a disadvantage to the employer, and an advantage only to the workman?
Some gentlemen seemed to be labouring under a mistake as to the question of an average or a minimum rate of wages, and appeared to think
that the rate of wages was placed at the lowest ebb ; but it was not—it
was placed at an average rate of skill. Some apparently thought that
the unions adopting the system wished to compel the better class of
workmen to work at that minimum, whereas they did not. In no society
that he knew of was this so. Nor did unions compel employers to pay
to non-efficient workmen the average rate of wages. The workman
was to be paid according to his ability, and if not of average efficiency was not to be paid the average rate of wages—at least, that was
the view taken in the society which he represented. (Hear, hear.) As
to the advisability or otherwise of admitting into societies workmen who

could not obtain the average rate of wages in their district, the only way
in which he could look at it was with respect to the success and advancement of those societies which had adopted the system. (Hear, hear.)
He would deal principally with his own trade—that of the joiners. If
they looked at the old, original society in that trade, it would be found
that that society took members under the average rate of wages—non-
efficient workmen. The old society, established about 1827, had now
about 10,000 members ; while the society he represented, originated in
1860, or fourteen years ago this very month, had at the present time, by
its system of government, as many as 13,000 members, and an accumulated capital or reserve fund of upwards of £34,000 ; whereas the old
union, by its system, had a capital of under £1 per member. He took
it, therefore, that the better system for unionists to work upon was to
have efficient workmen in their unions, and to refuse the admission of
those who were non-efficient. (Hear, hear.) It was an advantage to
the employer, for if an employer applied to a union for workmen, in that
case he had the knowledge that he would obtain efficient workmen ; but
if he applied to a union of the old description, he knew not whether he
would obtain efficient workmen or those who were below the average in
skill. (Hear, hear.) He might be suited, or he might not ; and in this
respect the new system was much to his advantage. Mr. Ward dwelt
on the subject of the separation of funds. As to a separation of funds for
different objects, if Mr. Ward would look over the statistics of friendly
societies in the past, he would be unable to show that societies by
adopting a system of that kind had progressed favourably. (Hear, hear.)
On the contrary, they had failed by such a system. If a society laid by
only a certain amount for, say sickness, when the amount of sickness
was exceptional, members must go without benefit or have that
benefit reduced ; but by taking what was required from the bulk,
the pay to the members at a time like that alluded to went on just
the same. (Hear, hear.) In every branch requiring special benefit,
the advantages of non-separation of funds met the question. The
law had as much right to parcel out in lots the savings of individuals, as to interfere with the savings of a body of workmen, who
provide their own funds and claim the right to use them in any way they
see fit. It had been asserted that unions could not, and did not, advance

wages. He thought, from the manner in which the subject had been treated by the workmen's side, that it had been shown that at different times unions had advanced wages. Take, for instance, the recent movement of the agricultural labourers. What advance would they have got but for the fact that they were united in the bond of union? (Hear, hear.) They would otherwise still be grovelling in the mud and mire, as in the past. The farmer and landowner would not have taken their case into consideration, unless compelled by the case being brought prominently before the public, and unless the public sympathy were obtained. So in other trades. That evening one gentleman had shown that a certain class of workmen on one side of the Bristol Channel were only receiving 16s. per week at a certain time, while by simply going over to the other side they could get 26s. or 28s. In the latter instance there was unionism, and in the former there was not. This showed that unionism increased the rate of wages, thus offering an inducement to workmen to go over and better themselves. (Applause.)

MR. W. G. WARD'S REPLY.

(Tuesday, June 16, 1874.)

Before entering on my reply to the discussion which has taken place on my paper, I must say that I have been much gratified by the courteous spirit which has been exhibited by the various speakers, and not less so by the intelligence and vigour of their criticisms. Of course I never expected that every one would agree with the whole of the views I expressed, and on the points where the interests of capital and labour appear to diverge, there is much room for diversity of opinion. If all were agreed, it would have been an idle task to introduce the subject. But it is not so, and as I understand it, the only object we all had in view was to develop conflicting opinions, and examine them, with the desire to remove error and establish truth. If we were examining an abstract subject in which we ourselves were not vitally interested we might have had less difficulty in being strictly impartial, but we have unfortunately had to deal on both sides with the disturbing element of self-interest. No doubt the immediate and present interests for the moment, of capital and labour, are constantly at variance, and it is the influence of this fact which makes it almost impossible for each side to view the question comprehensively, keeping steadily in mind the relative bearings of the interests of each side on the other, over an extended period of time, and throughout a successive number of operations. If the subject of capital and labour be looked at, as it often is, from the single point of view of one isolated transaction between one capitalist and one workman, the conclusion is inevitable, that it is for the interest of each to get as much out of the other as possible, and the result arrived at is of necessity that their interests are antagonistic. Some people seem determined to take no other view than this, and appear to suppose that by multiplying this one transaction by the number of all that take place they arrive at the true state of the case. The problem is not so simple; in fact, the deeper we examine, the more shall we discover its complexity. We shall find action which appears to tend to one result, in its reaction operating in an entirely contrary direction. This is often the case, both in nature, morals, and science. It is pre-eminently so in the science of political economy, of which our subject forms a part. In dealing with it we ought to be specially on our guard against not only the warping influence of self-interest, but the tendency to draw hasty conclusions from apparently simple facts. We should endeavour to keep our minds in an attitude of calmness, and be equally ready to receive facts which tell either for or against our preconceived opinions—in fact, without this we only waste our time and our trouble. (Hear, hear.) Probably when we have done our best, the very complexity of the subject will baffle us; and although we may correct some of our errors, there may still remain a large measure of doubt and obscurity. Throughout the discussion we have had numerous instances of conclusions drawn from one set of facts, which by the light of such facts alone, appear perfectly sound; whilst we have had quite opposite conclusions deduced from a different set of facts, apparently with equal reason, and it will be my endeavour to show the bearings of these opposing views on each other, and to indicate the way and the extent that they ought to modify each other. And I shall have the difficult task of justifying on the one hand that selfishness which prompts men to study their own welfare, and on the other the spirit of self-sacrifice, which is one of the greatest virtues that can adorn humanity; the justice which will not permit us to wrong a fellow-man, and the justice which leads to the self-assertion of our individual rights. In consequence of statements which have been made to the effect that the principles at the root of the science of political economy are antagonistic to the principles of Christianity and natural justice, it will be needful to show that they may co-exist with perfect harmony, and that a due regard to both conduces to the well-being of mankind. There are numerous minor difficulties which will develop as I proceed, and with which I will not encumber these introductory remarks. It would be tedious for me to go through the remarks of each speaker *seriatim*, I therefore propose to deal with them under general heads. In this way the subjects of the discussion will be dealt with

once for all, but the different remarks of the various speakers may cause
their names to be mentioned several times, according to the number of
points on which they have spoken.

The first leading idea to which I shall direct attention is that expressed by numerous speakers, that there is something wrong for great
wealth to exist alongside of great poverty, and the inference either stated
or implied that the very action which created the wealth produced the
poverty ; and further, that it was actually a sin to accumulate wealth
whilst poverty abounded.   Mr. Albert Richards complains that " the
rich are more numerous in England in proportion to the population than
in any other country in the world, and at the same time England was
the poorest country in the world ; there were more people in it that
were paupers, and on the verge of pauperism, than in any civilised
country."   He also spoke of "millionaires" and "superfluous wealth,"
and assumed that their existence is an evil, and that they are in some
indirect way the causes of pauperism.   The laws regulating trade and
commerce, industry, and enterprise, must have been all wrong.   I venture to suggest that if we had more " millionaires " and more superfluous wealth " in the country, we should find the condition of all classes
improved.   It is the "superfluous wealth" of a country which is the
life-blood, the very vitality, of its industry, and the cause of its prosperity.   If wealth existed for the wealthy only, its accumulation might
be an evil.   Happily, Providence has taken care that it is not so.   Men
do not save to bury their savings in the earth, and in these days of peace
and commercial activity all accumulations are used for productive purposes in one way or another.   No man's capital is idle, and none of it
is lost.   Whether it be used to make railways, to drain land, to build
houses, factories, machines, or ships, or in any other way, it will always
be found to take the form of wages, thus practically and really feeding
the hungry and clothing the naked.   There is in all commerce a law,
irrespective of the wills or motives of men, by the operation of which it
is rendered impossible for a man to benefit himself without doing a
service to others.   If a man saves a hundred pounds he does not bury it
in his garden ; he uses it to increase his capital and his income, and as
year after year his capital increases he goes on employing more and
more people.   If those so saving become so numerous that it is difficult

to find people wanting employment, they bid against each other for labour, with the inevitable result that the value of labour rises, and the profit of capital decreases. An enlargement of the national capital is the enlargement of the fund which supplies wages, and it is upon this that the demand for hands depends, and whoever contributes towards this assists in progressively increasing the remuneration of the working classes. But it will be said it is the size of individual fortunes that we object to ; we would like to see them in smaller amounts and in more hands. Well, I have no objection, provided it can be managed honestly. If it can be shown that the laws of the country can be in any way improved, so as to give all men more equal chances, let it be done ; but I am of opinion that the right of property to be held sacred is the only solid foundation on which human society can be held together. Any proposal which has for its object the filling of one set of pockets from the pockets of others, whether it be by the acts of self-organised bodies of men or by the application of a system of Communism to the State, can, I think, only end in failure and disappointment. Mr. Start has said, " The question of capital and labour is very imperfectly understood, whilst in this country thousands lack the necessaries of life, in the sight of vast piles of wealth and plenty." Now, as the only way in which wealth can be profitably employed is by its distribution amongst the people, on the one condition that they consent to be employed productively in return, I can see no remedy for such a state of things but vaster piles of wealth and greater plenty. In other words, there must be more saving. Capitals must become larger or more numerous. No amount of wild talk about the "tyranny of capital," " the just claims of labour," "a fair rate of wages," will forward the matter in the least. Mr. Morton said "each wanted sufficient food and a proper house to live in." If there is a deficiency of food and of good houses, it is a proof that enough work has not been done, or that consumption has been too great. I suppose no one will think that it is a desirable thing that capital should be made more directly responsible for equalising the conditions of men than it is at present. If so, it can easily be done by a process which would soon exhaust all the capital in the country, namely, relaxing the Poor Law to the extent of giving every one "plenty of food and a good house to live in," who has not by his own efforts secured these advantages, and, of course, taxing for the purpose all who have. I know it will be said such a proposition is absurd ; what we want is that the relations of capital and labour shall be so adjusted that this will be the natural result. Very well then, I will make another proposition : let everybody be industrious and frugal. I think men can help themselves, under present conditions, and that poverty and pauperism cannot be traced to the undue assertion of the claims of capital, as has been been said by Mr. W. A. Richards, but rather to the fact that the people have been disciplined in improvidence. No doubt it is very humane to shield people from the sharp penalties of carelessness, but the inevitable result of doing so is to make them less careful. In this matter as in many others, the immediate consequence of the act performed is seen to be the relief of suffering, and the remote consequence, that by the same act we stimulate the very course of action which produced the suffering, is often lost sight of. Mr. Councillor Parker, speaking on this point, said, "It seemed to him strictly in accordance with the nature of things that pauperism should increase in proportion as wealth accumulated and human sympathies grew." I think this cannot be true. Would it not be more correct to say that pauperism grew in proportion as human sympathies were misdirected ? (Applause.) It is lamentable to contemplate the fact, already stated in this discussion, that about a million of our countrymen are actually paupers, and about as many more are bordering on pauperism, having already been on the parish books, and will again sooner or later claim legal relief. This is a painful reflection, rendered all the more sorrowful by the contrast of wealth and prosperity, and particularly when we cannot doubt that the very application of wealth to such relief has been largely instrumental in developing the evil, whilst intending only to mitigate suffering. It is one of the most important social problems of the present day to devise means by which this may be checked. A very suggestive paper on this subject was read by Mr. Bartley last year, at Bradford, at a meeting of the British Association for the Advancement of Science. Its title was, "The Poor Law—in its effect on thrift, with suggestions for an improved system of out-door relief." He would make thrift in some way or other the necessary qualification for out-door relief, and would compel all who were destitute to go into the house, unless they could prove that they had practised habits of thrift. No doubt a system based on this principle would, if it could be worked out, stimulate all classes to acquire provident and careful habits, and in the course of time be the means of reducing pauperism, and laying the foundation for an improved condition of the wage-earning classes.

Several speakers suggested that when an employer found he was making large profits, he ought to divide them with his workmen. Mr. Richard Lamb put this clearest when he said, " Supposing, for instance, that an employer realised about fifty per cent. profit. If he took the whole of that, and at the same time gave a man whom he employed poor wages, though it might be rather strong language to use, he affirmed that the man so employed was deliberately robbed." I I think it must be a very exceptional occurrence, in a very exceptional trade, for an employer to realise fifty per cent.—(laughter)—but if he did, I cannot find any just principle by which I can persuade myself that unless he gave a portion of it to somebody else, he would be robbing them. A very prominent member of one of the largest trades' unions is in the habit of reiterating the statement that " A workman's labour is his commodity, and he is justified in obtaining for it the largest price he can get, just the same as a tradesman gets the best price he can for his wares." I do not quarrel with this statement of the case ; it is an intelligible proposition, and one which I believe to be perfectly sound and just. I cannot find a bottom to phrases such as " a fair day's wages for a fair day's work," and a " reasonable division between employer and employed." They are meaningless, unless some one can show a natural standard by which we may measure "fairness" and "reasonableness." In all businesses there are risks of various kinds, and very often serious losses, even to the extent of the ruin of the employers. Who takes these risks and suffers these losses ? Not the workman. He gets profits whether any are made or not. Wages are assumed profits, paid beforehand. The employer, calculating the chances of his profit on an article when made and sold, pays down a fixed and final sum, agreed on beforehand, for such services as he requires ; the workman in all cases selling his services to the employer who will pay him most. The workman cannot wait for months, or perhaps even for a year, until the produce or

the article is sold ; he must have his share of the supposed profit before
any is realised, and in the face of the possibility of loss.   If the employer
is obliged to take all the risk, I think he must be held to be in justice
entitled to the profit.   But it must not be supposed that, therefore, the
workman derives no benefit from great prosperity ; on the contrary, the
successful man of business extends his operations, and others from less
lucrative trades flock in to those which are paying large rates of profit,
an extra demand for hands sets in, and wages inevitably rise.   We have
all seen this again and again.   Here, as before, we may see that there
are laws at work superior to human wisdom, an unseen hand producing
the very opposite results from those which at first sight show themselves.
That which appears to be an injustice and an evil is turned into a blessing.   In all transactions there are two consequences—one immediate,
which is seen by everybody ; the other remote, not seen at first, and by
many never recognised at all.   Men often rebel against the first, not
trusting to the working out of the second by that wisdom which pervades
the universe.   It is the business of the science of political economy to
trace out these laws, to teach men to act in accordance with them, and
to prove that so far as they disregard them they are sure to suffer.
(Applause.)

Some of my critics have said something like the following :—" Look
at the suffering that exists; if political economy leads to this, I do not
believe in it."   This is as childish as saying, if people fall down stairs
and break their necks, that there ought to be no law of gravitation.
Men's opinions do not alter facts, and eternal laws will not bend to any
one's caprice or whim.   Water will not run up hill in the social any
more than in the natural world, and all the scheming that for thousands
of years has been going on, and is going now as much as ever, to try and
make things go right, apart from the energy and struggling effort which
is prompted by self-interest, is, in my opinion, as far off success as are
the perpetual motion schemers, who think they can defy the principles of
mechanics.   If you want results you must have a motive power, and
your results will, I think, be just in proportion to the amount of that
power.

My friend, Mr. William A. Richards, I think, is entitled to the honour
of having made the strongest attack on the principles of political economy.

He said, "In the past the sole aim and object had been, How can I aggrandise myself? not, How can I justly use what is put into my hands for myself and my fellow creatures? He thought that any consideration of this subject ought certainly to embrace the first principles of natural justice, and these did not seem to him to justify, generally, the principles of political economy, as he understood them—which really put into the form of a science the old couplet,

> ' He shall take who has the power,
> And he shall keep who can.'

He believed that this was a doctrine essentially consistent with the principles of political economy, but utterly repugnant to all principles of natural justice." And speaking of making money, "He believed that in proportion as we put out of sight this consideration, to that extent would the interests of others be advanced, and the happiness of all promoted." There is an amount of sophistry and plausible error in all this, put together with so much ingenuity, that it is necessary to examine it carefully. The whole error consists in setting out with the false assumption that the science of political economy does not embrace the principles of natural justice—nay, that it is opposed to them—whereas it is exactly on the foundation of the principles of natural justice that the entire fabric of the science is built. Political economy has for its especial charge the task of finding out how the wants, requirements, and happiness of the human race can be best met—how every one can have what he wants, without doing injustice to any one else—how the services of men to each other can be rendered so that all shall obtain the greatest possible amount of benefit. As at present generally expounded, its principles are based on free competition, on equality of rights, opposing alike protective restrictions in favour of either capital or labour, and discountenancing in every way any attempt of any man to live at the expense of his fellow-men. (Hear, hear.) It opposes right by virtue of service to the plundering spirit by which men would wish to live at the expense of others. Charity and benevolence may lead men to give to others that to which they are not entitled, and it is in many instances very noble to do so, but do not let it be said that "natural justice" requires this to be done ; that is a perversion of language, or a confusion of ideas. Labour says to capital, " Give me more wages." Political economy proves that industrial

M

capital gives it all, absolutely every farthing. The confusion arises from looking at a single labourer and a single capitalist. The single labourer thinks how easy it would be for the capitalist to give him a little more ; and so it would, but at whose expense ? At the expense of somebody else, who is probably receiving even less, or perhaps nothing at all.

This is a somewhat involved point, and I will illustrate it by an idea I met with some time ago in a work by an eminent French author. Imagine, in a vast and fertile country, a population of a thousand people, destitute of all capital. They must die ; there is no help for it. But suppose that ten of them are provided with instruments and provisions sufficient to enable them to work and live themselves, and also to re-munerate the services of 90 others, and no more. Then 900 must die, under the hardest conditions—the conditions of political economy, of procuring the services of the largest number of men which the capital can command. The competition of the 990 who are in danger of death secures this, and the capitalists make their bargain accordingly. But suppose they mingle a little mock philanthropy with their political economy, and acting on it, take to remunerating labour handsomely. Will they do good or harm ? They may give double wages. What will happen? Forty-five men will be better off at the expense of forty-five others, who will have to die. This illustration ought to show that the evil of low wages is not the fault of the capitalists, but is attributable to the scarcity of capital. Suppose the capitalists in this community of 1,000 people to be 100, 200, or 500, is it not evident that the condition of all will be more and more improved, that those who are not capitalists may possibly turn the tables on those who are, and forming themselves into a trades' union, may even dictate their own terms ?. But the same thing would equally happen without such an organisation, by the competition of the capitalists for their services.

The man who has his labour to dispose of thinks he ought to have a high price for it, so doubtless do men who have anything else to sell, and it is common to hear the remark that less than such and such a price is not fair. The buyers, on the other hand, ask whether other men will supply the same thing for less. If this system is to be abandoned, where are we to stop ? If men cease to endeavour to buy at low prices, and begin to prefer to give high ones, who can draw the line ? Production, instead of being stimulated, would be checked, and the channels of commerce would speedily be dried up, and every one would be a loser. Production, distribution, and exchange, as they now go on, are under the influence of fundamental laws, applicable to human nature and human requirements as they really exist, and political economy is the exponent of those laws. Ignoring the apparent and immediate effects of a single act, it looks at the chain of consequences which ultimately ensue, and embraces in thought and forethought the whole compass of effects. Instead of asserting that one man should be considered at the expense of another, it insists that each shall render a full service for whatever he receives. (Hear, hear.) If self-interest works out to the advantage of the world at large, then let it not be assailed by vulgar prejudice. There will be room enough for self-sacrifice as well, in a variety of ways, without confounding the spirit of charity with the principles of natural justice. The two work on different planes, and are each necessary to the other. They are the counterparts of each other, and the true conclusion is that if you would in any sense "live for others," you must "live for self" as well. The rational dictate is, "Live for self and others." In the distant future there will probably come a time when individual foresight and thrift will supersede the necessity for assistance; but, in the meantime, public benevolence and private charity have a noble task to perform. To ignore self-interest in the social system would be to legalise, to organise injustice itself, for it would be proclaiming that there are men born to render, and others born to receive, gratuitous services, and such a system would speedily break down, because it would tend to the non-production of the necessaries and comforts of life. As the ages roll on, men may learn to do their duty to society without any stimulus whatever, in which case the motive of self-interest would naturally die out; in the meantime, the Ruler of the Universe has established this motive to compel men to do unto others as they would have others do unto them. (Applause.)

I do not wish to be understood to say that there can be no injustice in the matter of wages. In speaking of general laws one is always liable to be tripped up by exceptions. I believe that temporary injustice often exists, but I do not think it is always on one side. I have asserted, and still maintain, that organised labour is, in my opinion, necessary to the due maintenance of its rights. In the past, no doubt, there have been many employers who have ground down their workmen unmercifully, below the legitimate market value of their labour, if they had possessed the power of helping themselves, and many are probably doing so at the present time.

Several speakers complained that I have not spoken enough of the faults of employers. Take Mr. Hemm, for instance, who said, "The paper dwelt somewhat largely upon the faults of trades' unionists, very largely upon the faults of labour, and very little on the faults of capital." Similar complaints have been made that I have not been more exhaustive on other points. I can only plead the difficulty of dealing with so extensive a subject in a short paper. I might speak at great length on the faults of capitalists—of frauds in trades of all sorts, especially of the adulterations of tradesmen and manufacturers, by which the public at large are injured and robbed ; but the one point on which I should dwell the longest would be the restrictive monopolies and protective systems with which the history of trade abounds. I should show that wherever a man persuaded the law to save him from the effects of free competition, he, in fact, invoked the aid of the State to enable him to rob everybody else. In the old days of class legislation, such frauds on the community were common. The people were subject to a constant system of plunder, and the law, which should resist and punish plunder, actually became its accomplice. I should take a similar objection to the same thing if attempted to be accomplished by trade guilds. Any artificial monopoly I regard as opposed to the general interest.

These evils, however, being very much things of the past, I certainly thought it more to the purpose to direct my attention to some of the efforts that have been and are being made to build up a system of protection around labour, and to show that less restriction would be for the benefit of all ; and as many of my remarks on this subject have been criticised rather sharply, I must take the risk of giving offence by going again over the ground of these so-called "faults of labour," but which I call "errors of trades' unionism." In the outset let it be distinctly understood that I am a firm believer in the advantages of trades' unions, if conducted on sound principles, (Hear, hear.) They can, and certainly do, obtain for the workmen the improved wages which are their due, when there is increased prosperity and a greater requisition for their labour, more quickly and more generally than could result from the individual action of each workman. In many other ways trades' unions are valuable, as I explained in my paper, and as Mr. Hemm so fully showed in his remarks.

Upon these general points we are most of us agreed, but not on others. For instance, the policy of the limitation of apprentices, I said, "was a direct injury to the community at large, interfering with the prosperity of the nation." Mr. Start opposes my opinion that the employer ought to have liberty in this respect, and says, "The trades think that the liberty of the employer here was their ruin," and asks, "What class of men, other than the working men, are called upon or expected to sacrifice the interests of their calling for the benefit of the community, or for the prosperity of the nation?" Mr. Lamb asked, "What could be thought of swamping a place with apprentices? For a man to be thrown out of employment in this way, he considered, after that man had served a term of years to learn his trade, monstrous." As regards sacrificing interests for the good of the community, I ask whether the interests are upheld by justice or injustice? Mr. Start in another part of his speech very truly said, "The vast masses born in this country were not asked whether they would be born, nor were they asked the condition of their birth and station. All had a right to live, and to live well and happily." How does he respect this "right to live well and happily?" By refusing to allow them fair-play, to go into those trades which appear most thriving and prosperous. This system of monopoly in prosperous and skilled trades has, I believe, prevented the due expansion of those trades, and been, to a great extent, the cause of the extreme poverty and pauperism in the less skilled branches of labour. Take the case of the agricultural labourer, who has been justly mentioned with such commisseration by several speakers. Would it have been possible for him to have been kept down at wages not amounting to more than a third of what was being earned in other trades, if he could have had fair-play to enter those trades? Too many men have had to remain on the land, because they could not get away from it into something better; and this operating with our Poor Law system, whereby the farmers knew they must either keep the men on the land or in the workhouse, has led to a neglect of modern improved agricultural appliances, and to the employment of a large amount of badly-paid labour instead. A freer system might, and probably would, lower wages in some trades, but the public would gain a benefit in reduced prices. Keeping wages artificially high by these or any other forced limitations is, in reality, taking advantage of a protective duty at the expense of other people. But I have another strong objection to the system of limiting apprentices, and it is that some trades which grow fast would grow much faster, but for this. How is it possible to calculate beforehand which trades will grow the fastest, and require the greatest number of hands? (Hear, hear.) This is a matter which would take care of itself. Prosperity in a trade would lead to high wages, and high wages would attract learners exactly where they ought to go, to thriving and increasing businesses, and to the corresponding relief of all others where an increase of hands would be an encumbrance and lead to an undue depression of wages. As to Mr. Lamb's notion of "swamping a place with apprentices," and throwing men out of work in consequence, I think a little reflection will convince him that this could not be done to a great extent. Apprentices cannot be kidnapped, and their parents would take care that they did not place them in trades or under masters who were guilty of this swamping, because they would say their turn to be swamped will come next. Further, what becomes of the idea that the skilful workman, who has served his time, can be superseded by raw, untaught youths? Either the skill is not required, or it is. If it is, the youths cannot do the work; if it is not, the high wages are being received under false pretences. Securing high wages by preventing other men entering a trade, is virtually confiscating wages which would, under a free system which recognised the equal rights of all, be paid to other classes of labourers; because a burdensome surplus of labour is artificially thrown into other branches of industry, the wages in which become as much depressed as the wages in others are raised. Individual freedom is necessary to justice in this matter of the disposal of a workman's only commodity, his labour. Unless there be fair-play to all to follow those pursuits for which they think they are best qualified, and in which they think they are most likely to succeed, it seems to me that the equal rights of men are invaded, and liberty is but a name.

The point that this and similar restrictions tend to the destruction of trade, by forcing up prices unnaturally, I shall speak of separately further on.

I have not dealt with the right of the capitalist to employ his capital as he thinks fit, preferring to show that such action is a wrong committed by one workman upon another. Mr. Start's way of putting his case was very dexterous, when he assumed that a workman was expected to sacrifice his interests for the good of the community. The correct way of stating the case would, however, be—the workman must not sacrifice the good of the community and the rights of others to secure advantages for himself.

Mr. Mather, Mr. Frank Parker, Mr. Chatwin, Mr. William Clarke, and Mr. Moreton, all spoke emphatically against piecework, whilst Mr. Woodhead thought it "incontestably right," and Mr. Hemm believed "piecework to be the proper principle on which trade should be carried on between employer and employed." It is true both Mr. Woodhead and Mr. Hemm made out a strong case against certain employers, but if the principle is right, the difficulties of carrying it out can surely be overcome. I give the trades' unions credit for ability to protect their members against injustices of employers under one system as well as another. Nothing can be more philosophical than Mr. Woodhead's illustration of a man's labour being the thing he had to sell, and his deduction that therefore it ought to be sold by quantity, the same as articles are which are produced by labour. This is another way of applying Mr. Macdonald's favourite phrase, that "a workman's labour is his commodity." If this is true, and I suppose we are all agreed that it is, upon what principle can it be said to a man, you shall not be your own master as to how much of this, which is the only property you possess, shall be disposed of by you for something substantial, which will improve your position in life? If one man can work quicker than another, or longer than another, preventing him doing so is confiscation of his superior faculty, is a protective duty levied on the strong in the interest of the weak, is handicapping the vigorous and energetic man in favour of the indolent and incompetent. (Hear, hear.)

The question of an average fixed rate of wages is allied to the question of piecework, and in like manner there has been considerable diversity of opinion upon it. It is quite evident that some of the unions are finding

out the error of it. When I look at the arguments of Mr. Douse and
Mr. Woodhead on this subject, I feel that no reply is needed from me to
remarks which have been made on the other side of the question. A
remedy will have to be found for a system which brings about "dead-
levelism" between the quick and the skilful and the unskilful and the
slow workmen. Mr. Start argued that the onus of uniformity of price
rested with the employer. He admitted that the result was that to meet
the requirements of the better class of workmen the price had to be
raised, and the inferior workmen were dragged up in value at the
expense of the employers. I will not argue as to the onus, it is the
practical outcome of the system which is the vital issue, and if Mr. Start
altered the word "employer" to "public," I think we get the case very
correctly stated—namely, that the inferior workmen are dragged up in
value at the expense of the public, and to the extent that this occurs in a
large number of trades, the prices of all productions and commodities are
artificially raised, every one has to pay more for what he buys, and the
whole country is placed in a condition to be beaten by its competitors in
foreign markets. (Applause.)

I come now to the very important question of opposition to the introduction of new and improved machinery. I do not forget that Mr.
Woodhead, in the course of his very able speech, said he thought this
charge was somewhat out of date, and "he considered it rather begging
the question to rake up old grievances." I cannot agree with him : the
opposition has only changed its form. Nothing so vulgar and so palpably
objectionable as the frame-breaking of the Luddites is now resorted to ;
the process is more occult and skilful—less direct, but not less certain.
When new and improved machinery is introduced, by which more of a
given article can be produced—say in some textile manufacture, where
the work is paid for according to quantity—what usually happens? The
owner of it tries to get the price fixed at a lower rate, but at a rate,
nevertheless, which would make it a better job than in the old. He may
be able to find plenty of men who would be glad to work in it at the
lower price he proposes to pay, but the men working the older machinery
say they cannot allow it, because if the articles were made for less in the
new machinery, their prices would be reduced as well. The consequence
is, that a manufacturer finds it to his advantage to work old machinery,

rather than incur the expense of new ; whereas, if he were allowed to gain an advantage from the new, it would be to his interest to gradually replace the old, and improve the situations of the whole of his workmen.

It will be said, probably, that even then there would occur a great evil ; because if each machine produced an extra quantity of work, fewer would be wanted, and a number of men must be thrown out of employment. Several speakers have touched upon this point, but I think Mr. Mather put it most clearly when he said, " As to the opposition of workmen in any instance to new and improved machinery, being against their own interests, an injustice to the inventor and introducer of it, and calculated to inflict a wrong upon society in general, he would say that if the workman was always to make room for improved machinery, it appeared to him that as machinery became developed men must move off, and that the world was for machinery, not men." This is such a plausible and common idea, that I should like us to give it our most careful attention. I think an illustration will serve our purpose best, and explain most clearly what would be likely to occur. Say that a manufacturer employs one hundred workmen to make one hundred articles, and by the invention of an improved machine he can produce his hundred articles with only fifty men. If he could employ the fifty men at the same rate per man as he had employed the hundred, he would clearly save a large amount in the production of his articles. For the sake of simplicity, we will assume that the new machinery springs into existence by magic, and that his market is limited to his hundred articles and cannot be extended. Of course fifty men will be discharged, which exactly seems to prove Mr. Mather's case. But what else happens ? Every week that passes by the manufacturer is gaining, beyond his former gains, the exact amount of the week's wages of the fifty men he has discharged. This seems to prove that the capitalist has gained at the expense of the workmen. Calculating the wages of these fifty men at 30s. a week each, he will be putting into his pocket, you may say, £75 every week of his life, and for aught he cares the fifty men may starve. Happily, this is only one side of the picture. The £75 will not be buried in the earth—it will be used all the same. The capitalist may possibly employ it himself, and employ the other fifty men to produce something else. If not, he will put it out on interest in some form or other, and it will equally be used to employ men to produce something. In either case, the world at large would be the gainer to the extent of the extra articles produced. The hundred men are no worse off, and more articles suitable to the wants of mankind are brought into existence, and the capitalist who invented the machine is a large gainer as the reward of of his skill and enterprise. But these advantages never remain permanently in favour of the inventor only. Sooner or later, competition interferes with large profits, prices are reduced, and the advantage of the cheapening process goes to the purchaser, the consumer, the public (including workmen)—in a word, to mankind. And now the consumers will save something, which can be spent on other articles; and the production of these other articles will create a demand for more workmen. Thus as machinery increases men are not superseded, but the condition of humanity is improved, and the march towards a higher civilization is quickened.

Another process may take place, and in the history of trades often has —namely, the cheapening of an article may lead to an enormous increase of the demand, and so give employment to many more workmen in the very trade where the better machinery has been introduced. But this may or may not take place, the other process is certain.

The motive of the inventor is probably a purely selfish one, but there is in this case, as in others, a mutuality of interest between the individual and society at large.

And it is deserving of notice, that the interests of the various trades are bound together, so that a saving in one acts upon the prosperity of all ; thus if the production of an article of general consumption is cheapened, and its price reduced, every purchaser saves something which he may spend as he likes—on better clothes, a better house, better furniture, more books, or a better education for his children.

When speaking of piecework, I purposely omitted to notice some observations made by Mr. William Clarke, because I thought the unsoundness of them would be clearer after the remarks I have just made. He said, " He believed Stuart Mill laid it down that there was a certain amount of work to be done during the year, for which there was a certain amount of money to be spent ; and that there were a certain number of individuals to do that work, who could do it by mechanical means at their disposal at so many hours a day. Take it that these individuals could manage to do the work by eight or ten hours a day's labour, if they came to have one-third of these men working at the rate of sixteen hours per day, there would necessarily be a good many others out of employment altogether. That was the view he himself held of piecework, and he thought it was the view which the unions had of it generally." I think Mr. Clarke must have slightly misunderstood Stuart Mill. It is not the quantity of work to be done that is limited : this depends on the will and ability of the workers, to do much or little. No doubt the wage-paying power of capital is limited, and more than exists cannot possibly be disbursed, whether the numbers of the workers be few or many ; but whether the wage-paying fund called capital will be increased rapidly or not, depends entirely on whether much or little work is performed. (Hear, hear.) The profit of capital depends on the quantity of work, and it is on the amount of this profit that the possibility of more wages being distributed amongst the workers entirely depends.

Ring the changes as you may, it will be found to impede the growth of the wealth of the community wherever two men are employed to do the work which might be done by one ; and apart from this consideration, there is the further one, that by so doing you do not cause a single man more to be employed.

Suppose that one man working ten hours hours a day can get a ton of coal, and you decide that men shall only work five hours a day, of course you want an extra man to produce the ton of coal, and you may think you have employed another man. But this is only one side of the picture ; now let us look at the other. The selling price of coal has to be as much more than it was as the amount of the extra man's wages, and every one who buys it has exactly so much less to spend on something else. One man has to have a pair of shoes less, and the shoemaking trade suffers to the exact extent the coal trade has gained ; another one cannot buy the new dress he would otherwise have given his wife, and the weaver and the dressmaker are the losers. The extra man in the pit gets his day's wage, but the consequence is, there is an extra man out of employment in another trade. At the same time every one's comforts— in other words, every one's wealth—is encroached upon. The man who would have had his ton of coal and pair of shoes, has only his ton of coal;

and the man who would have given his wife the dress, must sit by his fireside watching his dear coal burning and his dear wife in rags. (Laughter and hear, hear.) In other cases, the money which is paid for the extra man in the pit would be paid to an extra man to produce some article to be exchanged in a foreign country for sugar, or rice, or tea, or anything which men in this country thought they would like to have in return.

Apply the same process of employing an extra number of men to do the same quantity of work to all articles produced for foreign trade, and we shall in time find ourselves beaten out of the markets of the world by the competition of other countries, and some branches of industry may be invaded by the foreigner in our home market itself. (Applause.)

MR. W. G. WARD'S REPLY.

(TUESDAY, JUNE 30, 1874.)

THIS question of the loss of our trade is one to which we ought to give the greatest attention. Whilst I in no way recede from the statement, that "Wages ought to be as high as they can be legitimately and fairly maintained," I submit that it will be found absolutely necessary for the trades' unions to study the tendency of their restrictive and aggressive actions, and beware of going to such extremes as will operate in favour of other countries and against our own. There is an ominous import in such figures as have lately appeared in the Board of Trade Returns. Figures are wearying, and I will therefore only call your attention to the fact that in the first five months of this year our exports have fallen off, as compared with the same period of last year, to the extent of £7,862,873. In the flax trade, a few years ago, the number of spindles engaged in Great Britain and Ireland was far in excess of those engaged on the continent, but a recent return shows this order to be now reversed, and Belgian linen yarns are now sold in this country. Mills of all kinds have been springing into existence with wonderful rapidity in various parts of the continent, particularly in Belgium, Germany, and the Austrian dominions. What is the meaning of the panic in our iron trade? How is it that Belgian iron is not only supplying the place of ours in foreign markets, but is being imported and underselling English iron in the home market? Is there nothing to be learned from the recent failure of numbers of our iron merchants, some with liabilities to two or three times the amount of their assets. If our colliers and ironworkers, or some of the trusted leaders of their unions, would but go and see for themselves what is doing in France and Belgium, their ideas would speedily undergo a change. We must be able to hold our own abroad.

or we shall find our trade soon dwindle down to a point at which the present number of workmen could not find half employment.

I have tried to show that limiting production, or making it costly by employing two men to do one man's work, or in any other way, cannot increase the wealth of the community, and must react to every one's disadvantage. Preventing or decreasing production, in order to create an artificial demand for labour, is no wiser policy than it would be to destroy what has been produced in order to create such demand. Both lead to poverty.

I believe that wages may be higher in England than elsewhere, because of our natural advantages and the efficiency of English workmen, when allowed fair-play; but if wages are pushed so high, and the efficiency of the British workmen so undermined, as that our natural advantages are more than counterbalanced, we may bid a melancholy farewell to our commercial supremacy. (Hear, hear,) America, China, Japan, our own Eastern and Western dependencies, and even our colonies, will take care to get their supplies from the cheapest and best sources. There is no magic in the name of England to command prosperity. Its maintenance is our own task.

So far as our home trade is concerned, the various trades are to a great extent the customers of each other. Mr. Allcroft said, "It must be recollected that there had been a great diminution in the purchasing power of money." Of course there has. How could it be otherwise ? If everybody insists on having more for his labour, how is it possible that the products of labour should not become dearer ? The question of less labour and more pay, is not a question as between employer and employed, but between the producer and the consumer. The employer's profit will be regulated by the competition of rivals, and the extent of such competition, taking the country as a whole, will very much depend on the number and amount of capitals, and therefore on general prosperity and saving. If a man buys cotton to sell again, he must regulate his selling price by what he pays ; and it is precisely the same if a man buys cotton and labour, and by a combination of the two produces calico— he must sell his product according to what he has paid. Consequently, with everything into which labour enters, if labour be dear the article will be dear ; and so it has happened, because it could not be otherwise,

that working men have not benefited by advanced wages and less work
to the extent they probably anticipated. The process would work well
enough for a single trade or two, if all the others would allow it, but
when all make reprisals, they are simply moving in a circle, and eventually find themselves just where they started. All workmen are at once
producers and consumers. If wages are doubled all round, each will gain
100 per cent. as a producer, and lose it again as a consumer. It is not
the money a man can get for his service which is the real question, but
it is the service he can get back in return for the money—the real issue
is the exchange of services. If each got more money because he rendered greater service to the community, each would be really and not
merely nominally richer. If a man would obtain a large measure of
what is produced by others, he must produce largely himself, so that he
can, by exchange, get what he wants. Any system which promises results on any other conditions is delusive. If a man had to build his own
house, grow his own provisions, make his own clothes and shoes, he
would understand clearly that his welfare depended entirely on his own
exertions. Where is the difference when a community of men, by division of labour, work for each other ? Must not the sum total of their
joint welfare equally depend on the quantity of work done by each ?

The intervention of money in the process of the exchange of services
in no way alters the condition of things, excepting so far as by artifice
some may gain a temporary advantage over others. The true use of
money is to measure the relation of the value of products to each other.
If it were composed of medals inscribed with the words, " Pay the bearer
a service equal to the one he has rendered to society," it would declare
its true mission. It is a claim on the community in return for something
which has been given to the community. Mr. Councillor Parker objected
to my view that money was merely the machinery used for the transfer
of wealth, which I illustrated by a comparison of its operations with a
system of keeping accounts by marks. He very justly pointed out that
there is a difference between the two ; the money of modern commerce
being based upon a positive value, the value of gold ; and he said, very
truly, that if gold became more plentiful its value would decrease. Mr.
Parker fails to observe that his own view is based on precisely the same
law as the case I stated, the only difference being that he supposes the

supply of everything else to be stationary whilst gold increased, and I
suppose the contrary case, of the supply of everything else being diminished ; the words to which I applied the illustration being, " If everybody does less work the sum total of production is reduced, and each
man's share must be less." I was speaking of artificial arrangements as
to the quantity of work which should be done for a specified amount of
money, and my argument was the very simple one, that if each person in
a community rendered less service for the money he received, the money
would not purchase as much as formerly when taken to market. The
fact to which Mr. Parker calls attention, that there is a positive value in
money, is the very cause of the wide-spread fallacy, that consequently it
must, apart from such other conditions as I have been noticing, always
place its possessor in a position to command specific supplies of the
necessaries and comforts of life.

In its relation to other commodities, money may be likened to the
counters in a game. If you increase the counters whilst you keep the
pool fixed, or if you decrease the pool and keep the quantity of counters
the same, in either case the value of the counters will be less. If everyone who puts commodities into the general stock of the community
requires more money, those who take the commodities out of the general
stock will consequently get less in return for their money. I limit this
illustration of the likeness of money to counters entirely to cases of
arbitrary arrangement.

The function of money is to measure the services of men to each other.
Men who render a service to society take money for it, which they have
to give back to society for another service, and society cannot return
more services than it receives. Money is simply a facility for exchange.

A man who grows corn may produce ten times as much as he wants,
but he requires shoes, clothes, meat, salt, sugar, rice, and a hundred other
things. Of course, the producers of these things want corn, but there
would be an infinity of trouble in effecting the necessary exchanges in
proper quantities and in just proportions ; but having in money a unity
of value, by which all things can be brought to a common measure of
relation, everything is simplified, and each man can make his choice out
of all the services which society has to offer.

Money is only of value in proportion to the useful things it will command, as will be readily seen if you compare its relative value to other things in England and in California.

The question of the exchange of services by means of money in no way differs from exchange without money, excepting as to the facility which money gives to the process. In each case the parties say between themselves, "Give me that, and I will give you this ;" or, "Do that for me, and I will do so and so for you." The conditions under which services are reciprocally rendered vary ; and their values relative to each other, although money be used as the measure, in no way depend on the money. A glass of water is of more value in a desert than where it is plentiful, and where corn, or clothing, or houses are scarce, much money is required to measure their value ; whereas when, by the industry of a community they are made plentiful, the money becomes of greater value. Thus it is that a man cannot say that he is well off because he has obtained so much money ; his welfare depending on what he can get for it. A man must not only sell his labour or his commodity, but he must buy other labour or other commodities, before he can judge as to the profitable nature of the transaction.

Whilst pointing out the effect of artificial restrictions as to labour and wages on the general prosperity of a community, I do not deny the right of any man or of any number of men to regulate the conditions on which they will consent to dispose of their services. To do so would be to violate the principles of liberty. I am a firm believer in the soundness of the doctrine of perfect freedom for every man. I would have no limit to the freedom of any man to do as he likes, excepting when he would encroach on the liberty of another. Each should do as he pleases, on the condition that he injures no one else ; but even freedom manifestly requires that the right of one man shall be limited by the rights of others, and this brings me to the point, that although men may mutually arrange with each other as to how, and when, and for what they will work, they are utterly in the wrong when they attempt to over-ride the independent wills of other men, whose birthright of independence is as inviolable as their own. I do not intend to dwell at any length on coercion and interference with others, by trade unionists. I believe it to be a deadly evil, and a monstrous injustice. I am sorry to say I cannot agree with those speakers who have stated that such things rarely occur. (Hear.) It is,

N

however, gratifying to find so many intelligent men repudiating the principle, not only on their own behalf, but on behalf of their unions ; and I can only regret that all who have spoken have not done the same. Two speakers took an opposite view, and clearly laid it down that in their opinion the majority ought to rule the minority, whether the minority belong to the unions or not.

A man may surrender his liberty, and agree to be bound by the opinion of a majority of any body to which he attaches himself, and it may be for the common interests of classes of men to do so, but it is wrong for them to seek to enforce their decisions on others who prefer to act independently. "A workman's labour is his commodity," must again be quoted ; it is his only property, the one thing he has to sell, and he is entitled to decide for himself, if he prefers to do so, how, and in what way, and on what terms he will dispose of it. If he can work twice as long or twice as fast as others, he has a right to do so. If he can get more than others, or thinks it, under certain conditions, to be to his advantage to take less, he ought to be at liberty to do so, and he is not a free man if he cannot. (Applause) A man's time, and strength, and skill are his own, and if he chooses to retain his freedom, his right to work as long as he likes, and for what wages he likes, cannot, I think, in justice be denied him. He may voluntarily give up his freedom, but it ought not to be badgered out of him by harass, annoyance, terrorism, or any other interference whatever. Reasonable persuasion is perfectly ligitimate and fair, but that is a very different thing from making a man a blacksheep, and submitting him to a thousand petty persecutions, whereby his life is so embittered that in the end, finding he cannot have both peace and liberty, he chooses to purchase the one by the sacrifice of the other.

Past generations of Englishmen have waded through blood to gain liberty and to maintain it, and have even bought it for their descendants at the cost of life itself. It is the heritage of all, and should be jealously guarded.

To the extent that a man is compelled, by whatever influence, to surrender his independence, contrary to his own will, he becomes a slave, no matter whether it be to one man or to a thousand.

Liberty cannot but sanction voluntary combinations of men for the assertion, maintenance, and defence of their own rights; but it will eternally deny the justice of all attempts to annihilate the equal rights of men who do not choose to join such combinations. (Applause.)

And if every man is entitled by natural justice to be free, not from actual bondage merely, but to exercise his own powers of body and mind for his own benefit, it follows that property must be held sacred, because all property is the product of men's faculties and powers as applied to natural forces. Whilst it is true that no man creates anything, it is equally true that it is only by the efforts of men that the earth can be subjugated to man's service.

If the abolition of slavery, serfdom, and vassalage was the result of the recognition of the equal rights of all men to dispose of themselves—their powers and faculties—according to their own will, there was necessarily implied, as a logical sequence, the protection of each in the enjoyment of the fruits of his exertions.

The necessity of saying something on this point arises out of the discussion in two ways—from the way in which it has been assumed by many speakers, that those who possess property have in some way defrauded those who are poor, and from the distinct advocacy of Communism, the object of which was stated by Mr. Thos. Smith to be, "To confer on all men the advantages of civilization—the advantages of accumulated wealth. Not only so, but to insure to all through life that they shall not come to poverty as long as they do their fair share of labour, and in old age." (Hear, hear, from Mr. Smith.) Mr. Smith added that, "So far as the principle was concerned, rich men would not be compelled to enter into Communism. The application of that principle would be voluntary." But the two passages appear contradictory, the latter merely meaning that men may voluntarily enter into Communistic partnership with each other or not, and as it is very unlikely that the wealthy will adopt the system, and as the poor cannot, it seems to amount to nothing. (Laughter.) The former passage is broader, and asserts the general principle of "conferring on all men the advantages of accumulated wealth."

The first point to notice is, that before you "confer" you must *possess*, and to possess you must take the wealth from those who have it, which is commonly understood to be a process of robbery or plunder. (Laughter.)

Supposing a State to be so strong in the numbers and political power of its poor inhabitants, as that they could abrogate all the laws relating to property, and enact a law to the effect that it shall all pass into a general fund for the common benefit, doing so would be simply an act of wholesale plunder. Employing the medium of the law in no way alters the nature of the act. (Hear, hear, " The land," from Thomas Smith.) I do not wish to fix the onus of desiring to confiscate all property on Mr. Smith—he evidently would not push matters so far ; but when he says " he is an advocate both of the Commune of Paris, and also of Communism," he is playing with edged tools, and we cannot well avoid discussing the subject in its entirety, and as generally understood by large numbers of men, who wish to inaugurate a new state of things founded on the destruction of the individual rights of property. (Hear, hear.) Several speakers have intimated very plainly that they were of opinion that the possessors of wealth had not obtained it by honourable and just means, and that those who had none were entitled to claim a share of it. Mr. Mather's remarks on the illustration of the cakes seem incapable of any other interpretation, and a similar construction may, I think, fairly be put on Mr. Start's remark, that because "the vast masses born in this country were not asked whether they would be born, and had no control over the conditions of their birth and station," they " had a right to live, and to live happily and well." This seems to ignore the idea of parental responsibility, and throw it on the State, which is of the very essence of Communism, is subversive of the principles upon which our Constitution is founded, and would lead to a suppression of individual freedom. If the responsibility of providing for all children who may be born be thrown on the community, the community must eventually, in self-defence, control marriages ; and it will also dictate to the individuals for whom it has to provide, not only their station in life, but the amount and character of their labour. Mr. Smith was perfectly logical when he attached, as the condition of all men having conferred on them the advantages of accumulated wealth, the words, "so long as they do their fair share of labour." This the individual may not decide for himself. Freedom could no longer exist. Responsibility and liberty go hand in hand. If men are to be free, they must learn to take care of themselves. (Hear, hear.) If they throw the responsibility of caring for them on others, they become slaves. Establish the principle of dependence on others, and there must of necessity arise a controlling power, and that power, whatever be its form, becomes a despot, and the dependents are beneath its feet.

And if the condition of freedom is necessarily one of responsibility, I see no escape from the system of independent families, and the condition and station of the children in life must depend on those who are responsible for their birth.

This brings up the important question of "inheritance," about which I must say something a little further on.

In the meantime, let us examine the right of people who have property to keep it; and in doing so, let us not lose sight of the definition which Mr. Mather gave of capital. He objected to my definition, that it was "accumulated labour," and said it consisted of "three things :— land, minerals, and accumulated labour and money." Strictly speaking, I must submit to the correction ; but, in doing so, I may be allowed to say that I was quite aware of the fact he states, but considered my definition practically correct, and used it for the sake of simplicity.

If Mr. Mather expects me to draw the inference, that because the land and the minerals existed irrespective of man's labour, therefore men have no right to hold them as property, I must decline to do so, for the reason that their utility to man and their availableness for his service have depended entirely on human exertion, which has given to them the value they possess.

Who can estimate the generations of labour and hardship of every description, which have resulted in our fertile and peaceful England of to-day? Wild beasts and vermin, morass and bog, useless jungle, rank growths of all kinds of weeds, with no houses and no roads, are not an enviable inheritance. Those who think so can be accommodated even now in various parts of the world. (Laughter.) You may say it is impossible to trace out whose labour has wrought the change, and so it is, to do so right back through all the distant ages during which the work has been progressing. Conquest, the caprice of kings, fraud, and confiscations have no doubt often subverted right ; but that in no sense invalidates the principle, that the right to possession by virtue of human effort, is the foundation on which society ought to be built up, and on which its laws should be framed. Such laws have had force in England sufficiently long to make it tolerably safe to assert, that however wrongfully property may have been obtained long ago, it has most of it been disposed of by the wrongdoers, and re-acquired by those whose toil and savings have enabled them to get it honestly—by purchase.

· On the general subject of the acquisition of wealth a few remarks are necessary, because it has been stated that those who get rich, get so too easily. If this were true, it seems fair to assume that many more might do the same.

But the special charge that requires examination is, that the possession of capital gives a man an unfair advantage. I pointed out the fact, which no one has ventured to deny, that capital obtained a less rate of interest in England than anywhere else. Mr. Crouse and Mr. Mather admitted that this was the case as regards loan capital, but complained "that capital, when combined with labour, received more in return in England, if properly applied, than in any other country." This quotation is from Mr. Crouse, who added, "but he should say that the working classes did not get their fair share." Note the words, "if properly applied," for herein lies the whole secret. (A laugh.)

If the proper and successful use of capital in business were an easy thing, and the profits certain and as large as stated, would not every possessor of capital use his capital in such a way himself? Is not the contrary proved conclusively, by the cheap terms on which capitalists are content to invest or to lend?

Mr. Henry English asked, "Was it not true that men often started in businesses, of the secrets of which they were totally in darkness?" and said, "If a man were in possession of a few hundred pounds, he might employ labour and brains, which would carry forward his projects to success." Nothing could be more fallacious than this. All experience is in exactly the contrary direction. Capital in active operation implies that its owner not only labours, but that he knows what he is about. (Hear, hear.) I deny emphatically that capitalists in business depend upon their workpeople, and not on themselves, for subsistence and prosperity. If it were so, why should not all be equally prosperous, and especially why should any find themselves in the Court of Bankruptcy?

(Hear, hear.) Mr. English will probably decline to credit the working men, whose "labour and brains" are employed, with this disaster.

The fact is, a large business or a large manufactory is a very complex organisation, with innumerable details, which must be mentally grasped and worked out, at the cost of much anxiety and thought. It is essential to success in any large undertaking, that a man be capable of taking a comprehensive survey of the course of all his transactions, from the beginning to the end ; and he must possess a decision of character, which will enable him to administer and rule with promptitude and skill ; added to which he must have some or all of the qualifications of business ; he must be a man of observation, able accurately to study and to judge of the general course of trade and the state of the markets.

One man calculates all probabilities with such a measure of correctness, that his anticipations rarely deceive him ; another is never right. One devises methods of business and modes of operation which generally answer ; another is always bungling and muddling. One possesses insight and foresight and courage, which lead to speculations that turn out right ; another is all wrong in his ideas, or fails for lack of enterprise.

It is impossible for any man to foresee and calculate everything, and disaster and ruin may overtake the very ablest of business men ; but assuming an average of favourable conditions, the success of a man depends on himself. (Hear, hear.)

During our discussion we have had a somewhat exalted view taken of the part that labour takes in what has been called production, and very depreciatory remarks have been made as to what has been called the distribution of what is produced by labour, and especially as to speculation and bargain making.

Strictly speaking, no man produces anything ; he may combine, put together, and alter. He may convert useless things into useful ones, but the useful thing and the man who wants it must be brought together, and everything which is necessary to bring about this result is important to the transaction. Production, in any useful sense, is not complete until the articles required are put into the possession of those who require them, and all who contribute to this result are valuable in varying proportions, according to the services they render—whether the man who tills the soil, the carter on the road, the sailor in the ship, the worker in the factory, the proprietor of the cultivated land, the capitalist who supplies the tools, the cart, the ship, the factory, the machines, and the food and clothing of the workers of all kinds—the organiser, the inventor, the speculator, the banker, the projector, the merchant, or the trader.

This voluntary co-operation of all men, and their tacit agreement to work for each other on the condition of equivalent returns for services rendered, each man being the sole judge and appraiser of his service, seems to me to be the highest form of Communism—the only one capable of an application co-extensive with the human race, and the only one founded on justice and freedom.

It is the business of the law to secure freedom and justice, to give to all equal chances, to prevent wrong doing and dishonest acquisition, and to protect every man in the possession of his honest gains.

Assuming, then, that a man may possess property in his own right, as the result of his own exertions and abilities, it follows that he may dispose of it according to his own will. He may consume it, exchange it, give it away, or bequeath it at his death.

What are called excessive fortunes are, in most instances, not merely the savings of individuals, but are also the result of inheritance ; and I believe there is a feeling of deep bitterness in the minds of many whose lot is a hard one in life, when they see others enjoying great luxury and doing nothing in return—living, in fact, as is usually said, on their means.

No one can justify indolent, luxurious living on moral grounds, and a curse follows in its track ; but it is no justification for envy on the part of the poor, who could not possibly have been better off if the ancestors of the rich had saved nothing, and died as poor as their own. (Hear, hear.)

It is not by chance that men are in different stations of life, some rich and others poor—it is the result of positive causes, namely, the capacities and conduct of each one's progenitors ; and a man might as well complain of his bodily or mental powers being inferior to those of other men, as of the inferiority of his social position, and with equal justice envy another man's strength of limb, or vigour of intellect, or moral tendencies, as repine because of his possessions.

What is more natural or more just than for a man to leave his property to his son ? The fact of a man having a son is a reason why he should work and save, and thus the son ought, in a measure, to be the cause of his fortune.

From whom a man derives his birth he derives his patrimony, and I can imagine no just principle for Mr. Start's satisfaction on which men who have no choice in the one can have a choice in the other. (Hear, hear.) If their fathers have left them nothing, they must not set up a claim to be the heirs of others, who never knew them, and who had their own responsibilities to do the best they could for their legitimate successors.

But it is said these men consume, and do not produce—they are an exhausting incubus on the community. Some go so far as to say that though a man may have a right to property saved by his father, he can have no right to make an income by it, without work and without pro- ducing anything.

This is denying the justice of interest for capital, which raises the question of the utility of capital.

If capital is a power and can be lawful property, the use of it when trans- ferred from one person to another must have a value. It is not merely the daily services of living men which are productive of the necessaries and comforts of life. If it were so, all men would be much more equal from their birth and through life than they are ; but the truth is, we are all of us as much dependent on the services of the dead as of the living. What could we do without the cultivated land, the roads, houses, furniture, implements, machines, ships, and a thousand other things, the source of which goes backward not only one, but a hundred generations? (Hear, hear.) Legitimately, all these belong to those to whom they have been bequeathed. These things have been accumulated because of their value, and if they are loaned to those who possess nothing, they must produce a return. If a man takes consolidated labour from its possessor, he must give back actual labour. (Hear, hear.) The same principle applies to work and wages—they simply imply an exchange of the product of past labour for a certain amount of present labour, and the conditions of the exchange must be bargained for, for there is no fixed standard of natural justice. There may be large accumulations of the products of past labour and a small supply of present labour, or the reverse, and the conditions will justly vary accordingly ; but so long as there are men who want and can use to their own advantage what belongs to others, they will be willing to give a price of some sort, and that price, apart from any other service on the part of the capitalist than allowing the product of accumulated labour to be used by another, is interest.

There is no fixed or proper standard by which to fix the rate of interest. A "fair" rate of interest is as vague and unmeaning an expression as a "fair price" for a pound of meat or a loaf of bread. In either case the meaning is always inaccurate and transient—never true, and constantly varying.

If ten men want one house or the use of one machine, the capital embodied in the machine or the house will be worth more than if there were ten houses or ten machines, and only one man requiring them. Thus in epochs of prosperity the average rate of interest falls, and in times of adversity it rises.

Some people have a confused idea that if a man returns exactly what he borrows, the transaction ought to be considered as balanced, and so have objected to all interest as an injustice.

If capital were not a power, if it had no real value, no one would want to borrow. It is the fact of its power and value, which makes its possession desired ; and if he who is not its owner requires its service, he ought in justice to return a compensation for the power surrendered by another for his benefit.

A spade, a wheelbarrow, a plough, or a loom, are real powers, enabling a man to do that which without them he could not accomplish. They have not only a real value, but a daily value ; and it is the daily value which constitutes the claim of the capital embodied in them to interest, which is the price of the use of a power surrendered by one man to another, the beneficial use being given up by the one and transferred to the other.

To deny the justice of interest, is to say that twenty shillings given in twelve months' time for a sovereign received to-day, is as equitable a transaction between the two men as the twenty shillings being given at same time as the sovereign.

Those who argue against interest often say money is not productive, it cannot increase of itself, it is labour which makes it productive. This is to confuse real capital with money. That which money commands is the thing which is borrowed, and that has a real productive power when allied with labour; as may very easily be seen, if we for a moment imagine what would be the productive power of England if there were no tools, no machinery, no steam engines, no ships, no railways, and no accumulations of materials for labour to be employed upon, such as wool, cotton, silk, wood, iron, and coal. (Hear, hear.)

Preparatory labour is necessary to render present labour productive, and setting aside the intervention of money as merely a process in a real transaction, the real thing involved in every loan is the use of this preparatory labour, which being a service must have a value, or we get into the old difficulty that there are men who ought to give and others who ought to receive, which would give rise to the difficult problem of deciding who ought to give and who to receive.

If we are not prepared for this dilemma, we must not assert that the man who lives on the interest of his property, even if he does no work whatever, is living at the expense of others. His leisure injures no one, and envy is injustice. A good and wise man will use such leisure in a variety of ways for the good of others. He may be nobly devoted to the cause of humanity. If he is not, you can only say that he is neither good nor wise—not that he is unjust.

The pressure of the burden of interest may be reduced, but only in one way. The depression of interest is proportioned to the abundance of capital, consequently, those who labour upon materials, who gain assistance by instruments, who live upon provisions, have an interest in capitals being formed, increased, and multiplied, so that loans should be more and more cheapened, and their burden reduced. But so long as one man wants to borrow and another is willing to lend, there will attach a price of some sort to the service.

Capital is really a productive power, and will always command a share of production; no one can fix how much—an artificial standard is impossible, and would not be just. (Hear, hear.) The only proportion which can be asserted to be founded on natural justice, is that which is from time to time evolved by the conflicting wills and wants and wealth of individuals, freely arranging terms with each other; and times, places, and circumstances must have a controlling influence.

Having expressed my views on Communism as a State policy on the one hand, and of freedom and individual rights on the other, I will not discuss the merits of the various schemes that have from time to time been propounded based upon compromises of the two principles—such schemes as those of Owen, St. Simon, Fourier, and others.   Failure is written upon their history, and I believe that men must alter—human nature must undergo a radical change, to give them a chance of success.   High sentiments and noble motives have prompted such experiments in the past, and very likely will do so in the future, and not a word can be said against any attempt of the kind which is purely voluntary and not founded on confiscation.   For myself, I have no faith in schemes which propose to find bread for all mouths, work for all hands, capital for all enterprises, oil for all wounds, balm for all sufferings—in short, a provision for all wants, and an exemption from the necessity for foresight, prudence, judgment, sagacity, experience, economy, and activity.   (Applause.)

To the extent that any system proposes to supersede individual responsibility do I think it is sure of failure.

Natural justice seems to me to consist in the defence of individual rights and the securing of equal chances for all, and I hold that it is beyond the true province of government and law to undertake the equalisation of the conditions of men.   Their aim should be to secure justice, peace, order, and stability; to develop and organise individual right, and individual defence, the great requirement being that each shall so live as neither to burden nor to injure others, which implies the protection of person, liberty, and property—the three constituent elements of life, neither of which is complete without the other; and they cannot be secured or defended seperately, because the free use of our faculties is but the extension of our personality, and property is the result of the use of our faculties.

I regret that I have been compelled to state views in opposition to modes of action and schemes which are believed by many to be for the benefit of the working class.   I come now to the subject of co-operation, on which we shall be more fully agreed.   The principles on which the system of co-operation is founded are just, violating no one's freedom, and invading no one's rights.   No remarks could be more intelligent and clear on this subject than those of Messrs. Mather, Douse, Hemm, Albert

Richards, and Chatwin, with all of whom I entirely agree.   Mr. H. English, also, in his admirable speech, advocated co-operation, but he somewhat missed the mark by holding it out as a threat that it would be resorted to unless employers added a proportion of profits to the wages of those they employed.   He said, "He would recommend the plan of adding profits to wages to all employers, for if it was not quickly done, trades' unions would, without a doubt, become one great national federation. This being once established, co-operation would certainly follow, and would in a short time undoubtedly become a power that would materially affect the large employers of labour in this country."

Now, I have nothing to say against employers adding profits to wages in proportion to each man's earnings as suggested, if employers choose to do it, and I do not deny, that to a certain extent and in some businesses, it may answer; but I believe a far sounder plan to be that usually adopted, of remunerating most handsomely those who have contributed most largely to success.

My chief objection to these remarks of Mr. English is, that he assumes that employers are getting an unfair advantage, of which the workmen will proceed to deprive them, unless they offer forthwith this bribe of added profits.

I say exercise this power like men, boldly and courageously, and let the employers vanish from the land if they are usurping the position they hold, and obtaining unjust gains.   If employers do not render services to mankind equal to their gains, by all means let them be superseded, and the sooner the better.

The plan proposed is simple enough, easily comprehended, and I believe perfectly sound in theory.   Workmen have only to save money, start co-operative concerns, and manage them as well as private individuals do theirs, and the whole thing is done.   The workmen will have become capitalists, and being their own employers, they will, of course, take both wages and profit, and there will be no room for other employers —their occupation will be gone—and a grand advance will have been achieved in the history of humanity.   A peaceful and gigantic revolution will have been accomplished. No more will the cry be raised that the rich man grinds the face of the poor, and no longer will be heard the complaint, that the employers, the bankers, the speculators, and the merchants, are ogres who traffic in men, " who suck their blood, who eat their flesh, who kill them inch by inch, and day by day."

Mr. G. J. Holyoake, in a small work on co-operation, has said, "Wait no longer on the banks of the great and ever-growing river of poverty, for the golden boat of the capitalist to carry you over, till you perish. Awake to the fact that you may become capitalists yourselves— that you can and must help yourselves." I echo the sentiment of these words. Self-help is the only real help. (Hear, hear.) Independence is the glory of a man, and without self-help it is impossible. Self-help has been at the root of every emancipation, of every achievement, and of all progress recorded in the annals of our race. It was no fancy picture which was sketched by Mr. Henry English when he said that when co-operation was adopted by the trades' unions, " the vast amount of capital which is now used to support men out of employment would be thrown into the labour market, where it would receive its full benefit. And men, instead of receiving pay from their unions, or money to support com-pulsory idleness, would be contributing by their united action to the augmentation of the funds and the prosperity of their society." I repeat that " co-operation is the true beacon light on which working men should fix their constant gaze." The principle is sound and laudable, and worthy of every encouragement. Societies for mutual consumption, production, and credit are all possible to industrious, intelligent, and frugal men, and to the extent that they are formed and successfully carried out, will men really emancipate themselves from what so many imagine to be the bondage in which they are held by the capitalists and employers.

All who make the effort have my heartiest goodwill and wishes for their success.

But I must utter a word or two of caution against hopes and expecta-tions of sudden, rapid, and great changes.

If capitalists and employers have had gains too large, the co-operative system will undoubtedly in time be successful, and if, as many suppose, the management of business is an easy thing, that success should come quickly. But it will be well to remember that, so far as yet tried, the success has been rather against than with the co-operators.

The principle is certainly sound, but there are difficulties many and great to be surmounted. In this, as in all other matters, there is no royal road to success. The first difficulty is to save money, and no doubt it is a very great task, but it is the first step up the ladder. It is true, both Mr. Smith and Mr. Chatwin have advocated the employment of the funds of trades' unions for co-operative purposes. Mr. Chatwin said, " What was to hinder trades' unions from using their extensive capital in co-operative works ? The vast funds increasing year by year, were they to be wasted in fighting battles between employers and employed ? No ; for strikes in the past had been a loss on both sides, and what gain had been obtained had been of no account to balance the expenditure." I must leave it to the trades to study the wisdom of these remarks, observing, however, that the funds of the unions would go but a very small way towards superseding capitalists and employers, and that it would also be necessary for workmen generally to save systematically, and invest in such undertakings if they wished to reap individual benefit from them.

At the same time, I may point out that it is quite possible that a large indirect advantage may be gained by the establishment of a limited number of such concerns, because if it was found that they were able and willing to pay higher wages than private employers, no doubt they would, in the end, cause a general advance. Mr. Hemm quoted a case of a Manchester spinner who refused an advance, until a printed balance sheet of a Co-operative Spinning Society, at Oldham, was published showing a large profit, whereupon the Manchester spinner at once gave higher wages. Such a peaceful victory stands out in pleasing and instructive contrast with the miseries, the losses, and the heart-burnings of strikes.

And there is the other side of this picture. There are times when trades do not pay, when advances cannot be given, and even when reductions must be made, and if co-operative concerns existed in those trades the workmen would have a reliable guide as to what could be afforded ; in fact, I think it may be taken for certain that what they paid to those who were not shareholders in their own concerns, would rule wages generally.

The independent and the co-operative systems might exist peacefully side by side—they have both an equal right to exist by their own efforts, and that will prevail most generally which serves the public best. (Hear, hear.) If co-operation should prove the more economical system, independent trading will gradually but surely have to yield before its advancing strides.

But, as I have said, there are difficulties. There will have to be more mutual trust amongst men than, unhappily, now generally exists; and there will have to be, I venture to think, a recognition of a far greater disparity in the value of individual services than workmen generally are at all prepared for. The men who are capable of organising and carrying on such concerns will have to be more or less largely remunerated, according as the business is more or less complicated, and they will have to be allowed a large amount of liberty in the exercise of their judgment. Large committees or large boards of directors, spending a great deal of time in the discussion of detail and in mutual recriminations, would have but little chance alongside of individual sagacity, energy, and decision of character. Mr. Holyoake (in his book on Co-operation in Rochdale) gives some amusing examples of the waste of time into which committees may be beguiled. He speaks of a committee of thirteen debating for half an evening as to whether ninepence or a shilling should be spent on a broom; and, amongst other resolutions, he quotes the following :—" Resolved, that we have two cisterns for treacle, two patent taps from Bradford, a shovel for sugar and one for currants, and that the step-ladder be repaired." (Laughter.) "Resolved, that the grate at the back of the wholesale warehouse be opened for air." (Laughter.) "Resolved, that a watering pan be provided for the store." (Laughter.) Of course, these are very extreme instances, but they illustrate the principle of the economy of individual responsibility and liberty of action; and I am afraid it will be a long time before co-operation is on an equality with independent trading in this respect.

And then, as to the employment of first-rate ability, workmen, as a rule, do not acknowledge that it exists, and will be very slow to discover it, and exceedingly loath to remunerate it at its true value. Besides, it is probable that the most energetic and capable men will, for a long time to come, prefer a position of absolute independence, to being the servants of either joint-stock or co-operative companies; and as a rule it will be found that managers will not be so watchful and energetic as private traders. Of course, to the extent that managers were also proprietors, the stimulus of self-interest would have force, and to the extent that the workmen were shareholders and participators of profits, they would be stimulated to exertion beyond ordinary workmen, which would be a decided advantage of the co-operative system.

Until more experience has been gained and the system is more generally and fully developed, co-operation will probably succeed best in the least speculative trades ; those especially in which the element of workmanship is large in proportion to the value of materials, and where the credit given is small and the returns quick.

I see no reason to doubt that in time great successes will be achieved by co-operation, and that it will become a just and real regulator of the rival claims of capital and labour, and so promote, not only the material prosperity, but the happiness of the community. It is the pathway to peace in the commercial world and to the welfare of the working classes.

And let it never be forgotten that "knowledge is power." (Applause.) Mr. Mather and Mr. Douse both very justly spoke of the importance of education. As men become more competent and better fitted to deal with the varied departments of commercial activity, they will naturally command greater success.

In addition to primary instruction being much improved in the future, we may surely venture to hope that, in the interests of the working classes, schools for technical instruction may shortly be established in England, similar to those which exist already in many parts of the continent. And may we not also hope for the time when the science of life, the rights of man, the nature and value of liberty, and something of the nature of the intricate social organisation by which society is held together, may be taught.

In addition to knowledge there must be an improvement in the moral fibre of the masses if they are to rise. They must learn to rely more on themselves and less on others, and when they do this they will know, for they will prove by experience, that schemes and systems are of trifling importance in the elevation of the people, in comparison with what the people themselves become. (Applause.)

Social systems, forms of government, and codes of laws, are powerless

O

to secure prosperity and happiness, unless they are vitalised by national character—by the virtue and energy of men. Political and social arrangements may be more or less favourable, they should therefore be carefully studied in every possible way. Class privileges and class injustices of all descriptions should be abolished, aggression and repression being alike antagonistic to the equal rights of men; and such conditions should be secured as will allow each to carry on his life without further hindrances from others than are involved by their equal claims; and around all should be thrown the strong protection of the law, in the possession and enjoyment of all the beneficial results of their activities, which their activities justly and naturally bring. No matter what may be the name or the outward form of a system, that which is best administered is best; and thus it is, that in various countries we see the name of liberty paraded on high, only to mock the people, and the form of free institutions existing as fetters on justice and right. If freedom is to be anything but a name, it must exist in the character and genius of a living nation. It can never be the result of violent change or revolution, being a growth and development of the inherent qualities of the masses comprising a community. (Loud applause.)

The CHAIRMAN (Mr. Whitehead) then said that they were much indebted to Mr. Ward for the part which he had taken. The paper read by him had produced much discussion, and no doubt all sides would be perfectly satisfied with his treatment of the question. As Chairman, he had much pleasure in proposing that a vote of thanks be accorded to Mr. Ward. (Loud applause.)

Mr. WOODHEAD stated that he was sure it afforded him extreme pleasure, on behalf of his friends who had taken the part of labour, to second the proposition introduced by the Chairman. All would no doubt agree with him in saying that on this occasion the vote of thanks was not merely formal. (Applause.) The subject they had been discussing was one unquestionably of national as well as individual importance. To every one throughout the country, no matter what his position, whether employer or employed, or belonging to what was called the general community, the relations of labour and capital affected him in every walk of life. (Hear, hear.) However much they might differ on the details of the various phases of the subject, there could be no doubt that Mr. Ward had brought to bear an amount of research and study that had been instructive to all who had heard his paper, and to those who would read it. (Applause.) The fact that such a discussion could take place with so much courtesy between what he might term the two parties, was sufficient proof that the relations of capital and labour were on the way to great improvement. They should, in this matter, substitute considerations of reason and intelligence for considerations simply of passion and prejudice. Everything that could be done to afford and disseminate information on the subject was no doubt a step which would tend to facilitate that desirable end, and Mr. Ward was entitled to the earnest thanks of all who had listened to him, and of all who were interested. On behalf of the representatives of labour, he very cordially seconded the proposition.

The vote of thanks having been carried with applause,

Mr. W. G. WARD said it had been a great satisfaction to him to take part in the discussion, and it would at all times be not only a matter of pleasure, but he should regard it as a duty, to do whatever he could to assist in forming a correct and sound public opinion upon a question of such vital importance. He was sure that he had not entered upon the discussion in the spirit of a partisan, or with a view to advocate the class interests of employers. His sole object had been to do as much as he could, first of all, to make his paper suggestive, in order to ensure a discussion; and then, in reply, to deal with the most weighty objections raised, in a fair spirit. (Hear, hear.) He had not sought out those passages where he could turn a point against a speaker, but those which appeared to have principles involved, and which seemed to him to require explanation, and to be capable of some correction. He did not assume that all his views were correct, or that they were complete, and he did not wish any one to suppose that he thought so, for the subject was too extensive. There were a number of topics of which he had made notes for his reply, which he had been compelled to omit, so that there were points remaining unanswered.. But he hoped to have the opportunity of dealing with subjects that sprang out of this question—side issues ; and he hoped that now an interest had been awakened in social, economic questions, the workmen would pursue it further.   (Loud applause.)

Mr. J. W. DOUSE said he had the honour and pleasure to move "That this meeting, and especially the representatives of labour, accord our heartiest thanks to the Committee of the Literary Section of that Club for their kind invitation to take part in the debate, and trust that this discussion will be made a precedent for future debates which in any way affect labour ; and he desired at the same time to couple the name of thier valuable Honorary Secretary of the Literary Section, Mr. E. Killingley, of whom they ought to be proud—(cheers)—for the very kind and courteous manner which, on every occasion, that gentleman had displayed to the representatives of labour.   (Loud applause.)

Mr. LEOPOLD HAMEL said he had great pleasure in seconding the resolution proposed by Mr. Douse.   They need only keep upon the path laid out for them during this first session, in order to maintain the very high position the club had so deservedly attained.   It would be invidious to single out any one individual member of the Committee to which they were so much indebted, but he happened to know something of the duties of an honorary secretary.   It was no sinecure office, when faithfully discharged.   He had some genuine hard work to perform, of which many were little aware.   Mr. Killingley had cheerfully undertaken these duties, and, without fee or reward, had carried them out with consummate ability, tact, and skill—(applause)—and he need only point to the debate which they had closed that night, to show how much the members were indebted to him.   (Hear, hear.)   He had been their *Deus ex machina*, and quietly but efficiently assisted to place the Literary Section of that Club in its proud position.   (Loud applause.)

The vote having been carried with acclamation,

Mr. E. KILLINGLEY (Honorary Secretary of the Literary Section of the Club) said that, on behalf of the Committee of the Literary Section of the Nottingham Liberal Club, he was much obliged for their thanks, and was glad that the action they had taken was appreciated. Their only object had been to bring together the employers and employees, believing that by the interchange of thoughtful opinion upon this important subject, a broader basis might be laid, and a truer recognition secured of the rights and responsibilities of capital and labour. He hoped the interest would not subside that night—(hear, hear)—but that some practical good would be the result (as suggested by Mr. Hamel, Mr. Start, and other speakers), in the formation of a union of both " capital and labour," to discuss trade questions—not in the storm of strikes, but in the calm haven of industrial toil. (Cheers.) During the ten nights they had met in that room, he was happy to say that no sound of discord had broken the harmony of the debate. To Mr. Ward, who had so nobly come forward with his masterly paper and reply, he could only add a wreath of gratitude to bind the posy of his thanks. (Cheers.) He must also pay a deserved tribute of admiration to the very able expositors of the views of the different sections of the trades' unions and kindred associations of labour in the town, who had so frankly responded to the request of the Committee. (Applause.) Kindly mention had been made of his own name, but he earnestly assured them that his streamlet of contributory service had been most cheerfully rendered ; and he rejoiced that, through their co-operation, the first literary parliamentary session of the club had been attended with remarkable success. In conclusion, he wished them a pleasant vacation, and hoped to meet them again at Phillipi. (Laughter and applause.)

Mr. E. GRIPPER rose with very great pleasure to propose a vote of thanks to Mr. Whitehead, their Chairman, for the admirable manner in which he had discharged the duties devolving upon him. He had been present at every meeting, involving much sacrifice of time and labour, and he was sure they were all indebted to him. (Cheers.)

Mr. W. START, on behalf of the representatives of labour, said they had been treated most fairly by the Chairman during the discussion, and he seconded the resolution with much pleasure.

The resolution having been carried unanimously,

Mr. W. WHITEHEAD responded by thanking them for the vote of confidence. If he had given them satisfaction, it was his highest reward. He might say his duties had been lightened by the assistance received from them. (Applause.)

Mr. R. SANKEY (Bulwell, Notts.) proposed a vote of thanks to the representative of the *Nottingham Daily Express*, Mr. A. W. Hayes, for the verbatim, accurate, and impartial manner in which he had reported the proceedings. He (the speaker) had attended that meeting at some inconvenience, having travelled that day from Liverpool. It had been a source of great pleasure and profit to him, at a distance from Nottingham, to read the debate as reported in the *Express*. A more difficult and thankless office could not be imagined than that of a reporter, nor one requiring more skill in manipulating the remarks of the various speakers, and therefore it gave him great pleasure to find that Mr. Hayes, who was an old acquaintance, had given them satisfaction. (Cheers.)

Mr. E. KILLINGLEY said Mr. Hayes's ability required no eulogy, but having been intimately associated with him throughout that discussion, he endorsed all that his friend, Mr. Sankey, had said, and could bear sincere testimony to his ability and extreme desire to mirror the records of the debate as accurately and faithfully as possible. That he had succeeded so well, was no small testimony to his judgment and skill. (Applause.)

The resolution was carried with cheers.

Mr. HAYES thanked them for the vote of confidence, and was glad to hear that his services had secured their approval. (Applause.)

INDEX.

www.ingramcontent.com/pod-product-compliance
Lightning Source LLC
Chambersburg PA
CBHW020625030726
47497CB00007B/2416